HARRY THE POLIS
EVEN THE LIES ARE TRUE

. . .

HARRY MORRIS

First published 2006
by Blacke & White Publishing Ltd
29 Ocean Drive, Edinburgh EH6 6JL

Reprinted 2007, 2009

ISBN: 978 1 84502 113 9

Typeset by RefineCatch Ltd, Bungay, Suffolk
Printed by CPI Cox & Wyman, Reading

. . .

Dedicated to my late father
Frederick McMillan Morris
and my loving mother
Flora Lockie Morris

. . .

I'm Just a Man Like You

· · ·

This is a poem which, to a lot of police officers in the service,
including myself, epitomises what policing is all about.
I know for a fact that many officers retain a copy of it with
them at all times, in the back of their police-issue notebooks.
Read on and see why!

I'm Just a Man Like You
I have been where you fear to be,
I have seen what you fear to see,
I have done what you fear to do.
All these things, I have done for you.
I am the man you lean upon,
The man you cast your scorn upon,
The man you bring your troubles to.
All these men, I have been to you.
The man you ask to stand apart,
The man you feel should have no heart,
The man you call the man in blue.
But I'm just a man, just like you,
And through the years, I've come to see
That I'm not what you ask of me.
So take these handcuffs and this baton.
Will you take it? Will anyone?
And when you watch a person die,
And hear a battered baby cry,
Then do you think that you can be
All these things that you ask of me?

Anon.

Rambo

$\bullet\ \bullet\ \bullet$

During my probationer period in the police, I worked in the Oatlands area of Glasgow, which bordered on the infamous and notorious area known as the Gorbals!

Whilst there, I worked with an older cop called Geordie Gunn, better known as 'Geordie Bang! Bang!' He was, to put it mildly, 'completely aff his heid'! 'Puggled'! A 'total fruitcake'!

Now this was the opinion of every officer on the shift, but, being fairly easy-going and able to get on with most people, I decided to make my own mind up about him.

We had a few ups and downs during our working relationship, but nothing unduly worrying. That is, until our nightshift roster came around.

Now during the nightshift, part of our duties consisted of checking the security of shops and factories in our 'beat'.

As a pairing, one would check the front of the property and the other would check the rear. What you are looking for is any break-in or an attempt to breach the security of the property.

However, if there was a line of shop properties, then you would check the front and the rear yourself, doing each of the properties alternately.

One particular nightshift, about four in the morning, this was the procedure we had adopted as we walked along checking a line of shops.

I had gone to the rear of a property to check it and was coming back through the close to the front of the building.

As I did, I thought I heard something, so I quietly made my way out to the front entrance and glanced out and saw

Geordie, with his back tight against the building, peering into the entrance of the next close.

I immediately assumed he had seen or heard something, so I remained where I was, kept quiet and took observations.

Watching Geordie from my nearby position, he simulated taking a hand grenade from his breast pocket and pulling out the imaginary safety pin. He then appeared as though he was throwing it into the property's close entrance.

Using perfect sound effects, he made the noise 'Boom!' as if it had exploded and then, giving the impression he was holding a sub-machine gun, he jumped in front of the tenement close entrance and began making a shooting sound: 'Bang-bang! Bang! Bang! Bang! Bang!' Only he was more realistic, so it sounded like the real thing exploding and a machine gun being fired.

From then on I viewed Geordie under a totally different light and was extremely careful about coming out of any property entrance suddenly, just in case I surprised 'Geordie Bang! Bang!' and he mistook me for the enemy!! And shot me with friendly fire!

Morris's Safety Motto

• • •

'Feel secure at night – sleep with a policeman!'

Guns in the Family

· · ·

One day a telephone call was received at the CID office from a male informant who wished to remain anonymous.

The information said, 'There are several guns in the house at . . .' and the informant supplied the young detective with the address.

The young detective, convinced that the call was genuine and keen to make a good impression, coupled with a discovery like this, arranged with other armed CID officers to attend the house address with a warrant, to make a search of the premises for the alleged firearms.

As the CID officers made their final preparations prior to leaving the police station, David Turner, an elderly bespectacled uniformed officer, who was presently performing indoor duties as the CID office clerk, overheard the entire episode of events and entered the room with his gold-rimmed half glasses perched on the bridge of his nose, and carrying a copy of the public Voters Roll log for the entire area under one arm.

Opening it up at a page he had previously marked off, he handed it over to the eager young detective and said, 'Aye, son, your informant was spot on, there are "Gunns" at that address . . . In fact, there's an entire family of them!!'

Something's Missing!

• • •

While on police patrol at a busy shopping centre, I was walking about, speaking with some of the shoppers, when I saw a buxom young woman coming towards me with one of her breasts blatantly exposed and protruding from her blouse for all to see.

I reacted immediately and took her to one side and asked her to explain this totally unsociable behaviour.

The young woman stared at me for a moment, then a look of complete horror came over her face and with her eyebrows raised, she blurted out in all sincerity, 'Shit! I've left my wean up in the canteen!'

The Canine Family

• • •

On attending the report of vandalism to an elderly couple's home, I was informed that a neighbour's ten-year-old son had entered their private garden and pulled out some of their flowers.

He then proceeded to scatter them about their lawn and pathways.

I asked the couple if they had spoken with the parents of the boy regarding his malicious behaviour.

The elderly woman replied, 'No way, the father's a boxer!'

Quick as a flash, her husband retorted, 'Aye and the mother's a bit of a dog as well!!'

He'll Go Nuts!

. . .

During a refreshment period at work, one of the cops produced a bag of nuts from his food locker, which he added into his breakfast cereal.

'What kind of nuts are they?' I asked him.

'Almonds!' he replied. 'The wife was given them as a present, from one of the old men she looks after.'

Now, to let you understand, this particular police officer's wife worked as a care assistant to the elderly and made regular visitations to their homes.

With this in mind, I had an occasion to speak with his wife at a police function.

During the conversation, I was speaking to her about the almonds and I suggested she talk the elderly man into buying walnuts and that she give them to me for a change.

She appeared to blush slightly, before saying, 'Do you know the full story behind the almonds?'

Unaware of what she was talking about, I shook my head.

She then confided in me (I love it!) and related the following story, which she made me swear I'd keep to myself!!

Apparently, while she was visiting one of her elderly patients, he had asked her if she liked almond nuts. She stated she didn't but her husband was very fond of them. At that, the elderly patient presented her with a glass jar, full to the brim with almonds, to give to her husband.

Delighted by the old man's kind gesture, the cop had tucked into them, munching them while watching TV, eating them in his breakfast cereal, adding them to his

Indian curry; in fact, just about anything you could add nuts too, he added them.

The following week, on returning to the elderly patient on her routine visit, she handed him a large Galaxy chocolate bar as a thank you for the jar of almonds.

The old man thanked her kindly and, producing a full jar of sugar almonds, he said, 'I'll give you this jar as well, once I've sooked all the sugar icing off them!!'

Yuck!!

It's Yours

• • •

One day whilst working away in the front of the police station, the door opened and in came little twin girls, with hair in pigtails and carrying a small puppy dog.

'Hello there!' I said. 'And whose wee dog is this, then?'

Both girls answered in unison, 'It's weers!'

'We don't say it's "weers", we say it's "ours",' I replied.

'But it isn't yours,' responded both girls. 'It's weers!'

'Yes, I know that,' I said, pausing for a moment before continuing, 'but if you both own something, then what we would say is, "It's ours."'

Both girls looked at me rather unconvinced, but said, 'OK, then!'

'Right now, let's start again. Whose is the wee dog?' I asked again.

Both girls looked at each other for a moment, then replied in harmony, 'It's yours!'

Cell Mates

...

Whilst working for a short time with the Courts Staff Branch, I was detailed, along with an elderly police colleague, to form part of the police escort on the prison bus as it made its way around the various courts, uplifting the convicted prisoners bound for Her Majesty's Prison Barlinnie, or 'Bar-L' as it is known.

While we were performing this duty, an arrogant male prisoner, who had just received a very long custodial sentence, was trying to give the impression that he was a hard man to the other prisoners on the bus.

This he did by mouthing off at my colleague and me in a derogatory fashion, using foul and abusive language.

This received a minimal response of laughter from the other jail-bound passengers, most of whom were deep in thought.

At this point my elderly colleague, who was the butt of most of his remarks, leaned over him and said, in a very calm and assured voice, 'You have a good laugh while you can, son, because see tonight when I'm sharing my comfortable warm double bed with my lovely wife, Mary, you unfortunately, my son, will be sharing your hard single bunk bed with a nineteen-stone, tattooed, homosexual skinhead called Shuggie!'

Along with the rest of the jail-bound passengers, he had to laugh, but it was such an obviously nervous laugh, that I almost felt sorry for him!!!! **NOT!**

The Truth, the Whole Truth

• • •

A young, newly appointed police officer was cited to attend court for his first time in order to give evidence for the prosecution in a trial involving a breach of the peace.

During his evidence, the young officer stated that the accused had been bawling, shouting, cursing and swearing in a public place.

The procurator fiscal asked the young officer to tell the court what they had actually shouted during the disturbance.

The young cop replied, 'They were shouting that the police were a bunch of "effen bees", sir!'

'Yes, Constable, I appreciate what you are saying and realise that you are trying to spare our blushes, but I need you to tell the court the exact words they used,' explained the fiscal.

'They swore at us, sir!' said the young naive cop.

'Yes, we know that, Constable, but what I want you to tell the court today is the actual words the accused used toward you when they swore,' explained the procurator fiscal, who was by now becoming exasperated by the inexperience of his young police witness.

'They shouted that we were a bunch of "fuckin' bastards", sir,' blurted out the young cop.

'Thank you for that!' replied the relieved fiscal, before continuing, 'And did you apprehend them?'

To which the young cop replied without any hesitation, 'You're fuckin' right we did!!'

Window Cleaners

• • •

Walking through the office one day, I answered the telephone to an irate woman who reported, 'Somebody has just poured yoghurt or cream all over my bedroom window!'

On hearing her outburst, I offered her a solution: 'Well, can you not just go out and clean it off?'

The rather perturbed caller replied, 'What?! With a disabled son?'

At which point I paused for a moment, before answering, 'I think that's a bit drastic, missus. I was going to suggest a bucket of water and a cloth!!'

The Mimic

• • •

One day while out driving with my four-year-old daughter Samantha in the rear seat, a van driver came racing up on my offside and swerved in front of me, causing me to take evasive action to prevent a collision.

Receiving such a fright and forgetting for a moment about my young passenger in the rear seat, I reacted by shouting out at him, 'Away, ya stupid bastard!'

Suddenly I received a sharp reminder of my daughter's presence when she uttered, loud and clear from the back seat, 'Daddy! Don't call the man a stupid bastard!'

The Heilan' Coo

...

A few years ago, back in the days of the City of Glasgow Police Force, a newly promoted, young and ambitious inspector arrived at the Gorbals police station, like the proverbial new broom.

One day he called the older and more experienced sergeant into his office.

'Willie,' he said, 'have you ever heard of a female from the Govanhill area of Glasgow, nicknamed the "Heilan' Coo"?'

The elderly sergeant thought for a moment, shook his head and said, 'Can't say I have. Why, should I?'

'Well,' said the inspector, 'I have it on good authority that this woman is allegedly allowing police officers to use her house to drink alcohol and sample her sexual favours!'

'Och, I don't believe that for a minute,' replied the sergeant, rather dismissively.

'Well, that's what I've heard,' said the inspector. 'But we'll see!'

A few weeks later, the inspector received more information related to the inquiry he was making, and this time there was an address to go with it.

He rushed into the sergeant's room.

'Quick, Willie, come with me – I've got an address to check out. I think it could be the house belonging to the Heilan' Coo.'

Both supervisors left the office and made their way down the road on foot.

Finally they arrived at the address. It was a large red sandstone tenement building in the Govanhill area of Glasgow.

Confirming the address in his notebook, the inspector said, 'This is it!'

He was very excited and, as they entered the close mouth, he said, 'It's on the first landing to the right, Willie.'

As they approached, the inspector knocked on the door.

Then a moment or two passed before the door was eventually opened by a small, dirty-faced little boy who, on seeing the police officers standing there, stood staring back at them.

Then a female voice, with a South Uist accent, called out from inside the house, 'Well, who is it, William?'

To which the small boy replied, 'It's Uncle Willie wi' another wan o' his pals!!!'

What's in a Name?

• • •

As a uniformed officer, I was walking along the corridors of police headquarters when I saw, approaching from the opposite direction, an old colleague who had been recently promoted to chief inspector.

This was an old friend with whom I had joined the City of Glasgow force and worked with when we were both probationary constables.

As we got closer, I put my hand out to greet him and said, 'Hello, Ricky, how are you doing?'

Slightly embarrassed by my greeting, he looked around to check if anyone had heard me and said, 'If you don't mind, Harry, don't call me Ricky!'

Disgusted by this reaction, I retorted, 'Why? Have you changed your name?' Dick!

R.U. FEELING EXHAUSTED KNACKERED SUICIDAL DEPRESSED SHOCKED AND TOTALLY SCUNNERED?

THEN THERE'S A CAREER FOR YOU WITH

THE POLICE!

Short Cut

• • •

A group of workmen arrived at a police station in Pollokshaws to install a complete new central heating system.

All day they beavered away, ripping out the old heating system and fitting the new slimline white radiators to the walls.

Next, they measured and cut all the required copper piping to the exact sizes, in preparation for the following day when they returned. Then all that was needed would be to connect the exact measured copper pipes to the new central heating radiators . . . Wrong!

During the night, some of the officers on nightshift decided to try out the fancy little pipe-cutting machine, which the workmen had carelessly left out.

One at a time, each officer on the shift had a go at cutting an inch off all the copper piping left lying around the office . . . Great fun!

However, the next day there was total confusion in the office as the workmen tried to fit the meticulously measured cut pipes, only to discover that every one was exactly one inch short!

Needless to say, nobody in the station dared to put them wise as to how such an error could possibly have been made by professional workmen.

As for all the cut pieces of copper piping: well, allegedly they were discarded in the River Clyde some time during the night, when one of the 'police plumbers' realised the extent of what they had done!

Fishing for Jaws

. . .

When I was a student at the Police College, Tulliallan, in pride of place was a fantastic six-foot tropical fish tank, containing a wide variety of extremely colourful specimens of different shapes and sizes.

This wonderful focal point of attention took centre stage in the main entrance of the college 'Crush Hall', for all to admire.

At that time, my father was a keen enthusiast of keeping tropical fish. I was informing the college sergeant who had accepted the responsibility of looking after the maintenance of the tank of this as he was busily feeding the fish.

'Well, if he ever has an abundance of fish, tell him I'll accept any surplus he has for our showpiece aquarium!' he said.

With this in mind, the following weekend, whilst visiting my parents, I told my father about the college aquarium and the request for any surplus fish for their impressive tank.

As it was, he did have some surplus fish and supplied me with three large tropical species called 'Oscars'!

With the fish packed safely in a double layer of polythene bags and wrapped in towels to keep the heat in, I made my way back to the police college on the Sunday evening.

On my arrival, I immediately went to the police instructors' office, looking for Sergeant Lancaster in order to present him with the Oscars to add to his impressive array of tropical fish.

However, I was informed he would not be returning to the college until the following morning.

Armed with my bag of Oscars, I went to the Crush Hall and, opening the tank hood, I placed the bag in the aquarium water, in order to acclimatise the Oscars to their new surroundings.

Later the same evening, before I retired to my dormitory for the night, I returned to the aquarium and, opening the bags, I introduced the Oscars into their new abode.

I watched for several minutes as the new arrivals swam around the aquarium, surveying every inch of their new home as they settled in.

Next morning, I arose and headed down to the dining hall for my breakfast, convinced that my contribution had earned me some much-needed brownie points at the police college and that the fish would be a good addition and a pleasant surprise for the entire college staff.

En route, I met Sergeant Lancaster in the corridor as he was arriving and informed him of my new introductions to his showpiece tropical fish aquarium.

'Great stuff, Morris!' he said. 'I'll check them out after!'

A short time later, halfway through my cornflakes and kippers, I swear the college building shook as a voice screamed out, '*Morris!* Where are you?'

Not the cheery voice I expected to hear. I looked over towards the door to see a very irate Sergeant Lancaster enter the dining room with steam blowing out of his ears.

Lancaster by name and Lancaster by nature! This guy was flying!

What's wrong? I asked myself.

Apparently the new arrivals which I had introduced to his prized aquarium . . . had massacred and subsequently eaten most of his aquatic fish stock during the night and what they didn't eat they maimed or killed for later, leaving the tank resembling a scene from the Amity beach resort in the film *Jaws*!

Which reminds me of a quick joke:

Q: How did they know that the girl in *Jaws* had dandruff?

A: Because she left her Head and Shoulders on the beach!

(OK! OK! It was funny at the time.)

Anyway, there were wee bits of fishy heads, tails, parts of fins and bodies discarded everywhere, floating about the tank.

'What the hell did you put in my beautiful aquarium? It looks like it has been blown up!' he asked, trying to curb his obvious anger, as his 'pride and joy' showpiece and main foyer focal point was reduced to what could only be described as a battlefield.

As I stood there, trying to summon up an acceptable answer, my nerves got the better of me and I couldn't prevent myself from laughing hysterically, as I watched one of my fishy friends swimming effortlessly past with a large angelfish dangling out of the side of its mouth.

As for Sergeant Lancaster, he didn't see the funny side and stormed off to his office. The alternative would have been to batter me or give me a right good dressing-down, I think!

For the rest of my time at the college, I had to maintain a very low profile when around him.

I also had to endure the endless jokes.

'Hey, Morris, I've got an aquarium at home – can you "fillet"?'

'Good "Cod", Morris, there's something "fishy" about you!'

And my particular favourite, 'Hey, Harry, I heard you went out with a mermaid to a crustacean disco and pulled a "mussel"!'

With regards to the trio of Oscar fish, well, suffice to say they went on to clean up and lived happily ever after, in the showpiece aquarium, in the Crush Hall at the police college in Tulliallan. Alone.

They also continued to grow very big on their seafood diet.

With my intervention and influence, it became a much safer 'plaice' to be!

However, I'm reliably informed that, since I left the Tulliallan Police College, there's been a remake of the *Codfather* with 'Marlin' Brando!

'Fins' just ain't what they used to be!

Speed Camera Excuses
• • •

'I was en route to my nephew's wedding and was being followed to the church by a friend, the official wedding photographer. As we were running slightly late, I saw the flash and I just assumed it was him trying out his camera, in order to be prepared to start photographing the bride and groom on his arrival. Therefore I refute any allegation that I was speeding.'

Peek-a-Boo!
...

Big Alex Morgan was a colleague of mine from our days in the traffic department and he had two young daughters.

One of them, Suzanne, who was about three years old at the time, was going through a phase where she would lift up her mum's dress or skirt and try to look under. (Obviously been watching her dad Alex!)

Anyway, one day Alex was out with Suzanne, travelling on a bus and there was standing room only!

While Alex stood there with one hand holding Suzanne and the other on the passenger rail, Suzanne decided to have a look under the skirt of a woman who was standing next to them, facing the opposite way.

Just as she lifted the woman's skirt up, Alex looked down, spotted her and pulled her hand away, taking her to the other side of him. But as he did so, the woman's skirt creased and stayed up at the back, so Alex, being a gentleman, tried to right the wrongdoing of his daughter and bent over behind the woman.

He then, ever so gently, tried to turn her skirt hem back down.

However, just as he bent over his 6 feet 4 inches of gangly body to do so, the woman, obviously feeling something, turned around and caught him in the compromising position, with his hand touching her skirt.

The woman stared down at Alex in his present position with a look of utter disgust.

As for Alex?

Well, red-faced and totally embarrassed about the entire episode, he tried in vain to explain and convey apologies for his daughter's behaviour. But having looked at Suzanne's angelic and innocent little face, I doubt very much if the woman ever believed him!

The Pacemaker
· · ·

Mrs Brown was the mother-in-law of my brother Allan and she stayed with him and his wife Mary for many, many years.

She had been a healthy woman for most of her life, but several years before she died, she was beginning to experience tiredness and breathing problems.

Her sons and daughters convinced her she would have to go and see the doctor and a consultation was arranged.

After the doctor's examination, it was his diagnosis that Mrs Brown required an operation to have a pacemaker fitted.

This did not agree well with the ninety-two-year-old Mrs Brown, who had only ever been in a hospital when visiting family or friends.

Her son Willie sat down with her one day and explained that it wasn't a major operation any more and many people had the operation performed and went on to enjoy a much healthier lifestyle.

She sat digesting all the pros for having such an operation done and asked Willie, 'And how long will this "pacemaker" thing last, after it's fitted?'

'It'll last at least fifteen years, Mum,' replied an excited Willie.

She paused for a moment before blurting out, in all sincerity, 'Ah knew it! That would mean I'd need to go back in and have it done all over again!'

Night Out, Now and Again

...

I worked with big David Toner who, when off duty, became a good friend of mine and we would socialise regularly.

One night David and his wife were over at my house for a meal and a few drinks.

During the evening my kids had joined us, prior to going to bed, and Samantha, my eldest daughter, asked, 'Uncle David, do you drink every night?'

'Don't be silly, darling,' David replied. 'Apart from the fact that I couldn't afford it, your Aunt Margaret wouldn't allow me to.'

'Well, how often do you drink, then?' she asked him.

'Let me think!' said David, rubbing his chin. 'On a Monday, I go to the police club to play darts . . . and I'll maybe have two or three pints . . . just to steady the nerves. Then, on Tuesday, I play billiards at the British Legion Club and I'll have a couple of pints of Guinness. It's good in there . . . Wednesday, I'll go to the football and maybe have one or two pints . . . to celebrate or commiserate, depending on the result of the game . . . Thursday, I'll stay in with your Aunt Margaret and relax with a few gin and tonics . . . Friday, now that's my snooker club night, so I'll go for a pint or two afterwards . . . Saturday is my day at the horse racing so I'll usually have a bet on a few horses and afterwards, win or lose, I'll have a right good bevvy of gin and tonics, washed down with a few beers . . . Then, finally, on Sunday I usually stay in with a carry out and watch the highlights of the rugby on television. So the answer to your question, Samantha, is probably "yes"! But, in saying that, you would have to agree I do like my sport!!'

Ye Cannae Park
That There!

...

Working with the City of Glasgow police, I met and got to know many true characters – none more of a character than Big Willie Irvine.

Willie was a big man in every sense of the word and lived in the Bridgeton area of Glasgow, where a 'square go' was a semi-organised, bare-knuckle fist fight between two men, without the use of weapons.

Now this was unfair because Big Willie had hands like shovels and was built like a brick shithouse and, with these attributes, it is safe to say, he didn't have a lot of enemies. Mind you, those who were he just battered!

Suffice to say most of the people who knew him decided it was better to be regarded as his friend and keep him on their side.

One afternoon, while out on a drinking binge, or pub crawl as they say in Glasgow, Willie found himself in the wrong area – in the old Dalriada Hotel in Edinburgh Road, Glasgow – as the demon drink took its toll.

Unaware of Willie's reputation and, to a certain extent, slightly blind as to his physique, some of the local young bucks – having downed a pint of the local 'snakebite' (cloudy lager) and having 'sniffed' the barmaid's apron to top up their own individual 'bravado' – began to throw their weight about, amongst the assembled drinkers in the pub, including Willie, and even had the audacity to direct some verbal abuse his way.

Not a man to take this lying down, Willie responded with his own brand of retaliatory verbal abuse, but the young bucks became one too many for him to challenge (they numbered nine or ten in all).

Outnumbered, even with his physical presence and reputation, Willie left the pub under a barrage of abusive verbal remarks.

However, retreat is not a word you'll find in Willie's limited vocabulary and he was not about to let it drop.

A short time later, Willie appeared at his brother's house, asking to borrow his car.

He gave the excuse of having an errand to run.

Willie's brother relented under the constant persuasive pressure and reluctantly handed Willie the keys to his car.

'Armed' with a motor vehicle – and I use that word literally – Willie drove off.

After several minutes of continuous driving, Willie turned on to Edinburgh Road and made his way towards the Dalriada Hotel.

Almost parallel with the Dalriada entrance, Willie turned a sharp left on to the footpath, straight across the grassed area in front of the hotel, and accelerated, driving his brother's car straight through the double-door entrance of the public bar, sending tables, chairs, drinks, drunks, punters and debris sprawling helplessly across the barroom floor.

Others in the bar area ran for cover as their eyes popped in total shock and disbelief at the impact and destruction created by Willie's actions.

However, unfortunately for Willie, as he tried to exit the car in order to wreak havoc and more physical damage on the patrons of the Dalriada Hotel, he found the car doors were wedged in the doorway entrance, making it impossible even for Willie to force them open.

As he huffed and puffed, trying repeatedly to get out, it became obvious to the fleeing patrons that he was stuck and they quickly rounded on the car, like a hungry pack of wolves.

As they pounded bar stools and broken chairs on the laminated windscreen, trying to gain access to Willie, he was inside kicking the rear window out of the car, in an attempt to make good his escape.

Just as Willie hauled his large frame through the space and crawled out across the boot lid of the car, he was promptly arrested by the local police, who were responding to an emergency call reporting the entire incident.

Willie's unbelievable Evel Knievel stunt had prompted a quicker than usual response from the local cops, all wanting to see this for themselves!

Whether Willie was fortunate to have the police presence, or the local young bucks were saved the ultimate embarrassment of being beaten to a pulp by a Glasgow hard man with a reputation to back it up, we'll never know.

I have my own opinion of what the outcome would be!

Subsequently, Big Willie expected and received a custodial sentence for his reckless actions, but I can still remember him saying to me, 'If you can't do the time, then don't do the crime!'

I personally think that is sound advice to anybody thinking about a career in crime!

What a pity we could not employ Big Willie to enforce it!

All Bets Are Off!

• • •

'Tank', the likeable rogue from the Bridgeton area of Glasgow, received some unexpected bad news when visiting the Cardiology Department of the Royal Infirmary for a check-up.

It appeared he required immediate triple heart bypass surgery and the doctor wanted him admitted soon.

Tank informed some of his friends of the news and the following is the reaction he received from his old Bridgeton buddies.

'Can I get your car, seeing that you'll probably die during the operation?' remarked Wee Dougie.

'Naw, I won't!' replied a confident Tank.

'Ye might – it's a big operation, that bypass,' came back Dougie.

'Nae chance!' said Tank. 'I'm as strong as a horse.'

'Right then!' said Dougie. 'I'll bet you ye die in the theatre.'

'I'll bet ye I friggin' don't!' replied Tank.

'Right, ye're on. How much?' enquired Dougie.

'I'll bet ye a tenner!' said Tank.

They both licked their thumbs and rubbed them together, sealing the £10 bet.

A couple of days later, Tank was admitted to hospital and underwent his triple bypass operation.

Afterwards, he was wheeled out into recovery before being admitted to the intensive-care unit for observations.

Wee Dougie, on hearing that Tank had gone through his operation, contacted Tank's wife and enquired how he was and if he could visit him in hospital.

He was informed that the operation had gone well and

that Tank was in the ICU, but visiting was restricted to close family members only.

Wee Dougie was concerned about his good friend and decided to con his way into the ward, to pay Tank a visit.

As he arrived at the ICU, he informed the nursing staff that he was there to visit his brother and was directed down to the far end of the ward, where Tank was situated.

Dougie, slightly apprehensive as to how his old friend would be, began his slow walk down the ward towards Tank.

As he got closer to the bed, he could see several metal stands and bright monitors around it, with various tubes leading from them into Tank, who was lying with his head to one side and his eyes closed, apparently asleep.

On seeing all this highly technical monitoring equipment, Dougie nervously bent over the hospital bed to look at Tank's face and, as he did, Tank opened one eye, looked straight at Dougie, put his hand out in front of him and said, with total conviction, 'Tenner!!'

Friends Reunited

...

I was asked recently if I had ever gone online and visited the Friends Reunited website to find out the whereabouts of, and maybe recognise and correspond with, some of my old schoolfriends.

I responded that I had no need to visit the site, as I worked in crime intelligence and had first-hand knowledge of where most of them were!

Road Accident Excuses

• • •

'I had been shopping for house plants all day and was on my way home. As I approached the intersection, a large hedgerow sprang up, obscuring my vision and I collided with another car which I did not see!'

No Complaints

• • •

A young policewoman was attending an officer safety training course in the police training centre.

During the day she was paired off with an inspector in order to demonstrate her self-defence moves.

Whilst engaged in this exercise, the inspector accidentally struck her on the head with a plastic training baton, whereby the policewoman sustained a slight bruise to her head.

After receiving some first aid she was able to continue with her training course.

Several days later, the inspector was engaged in the front office of a crowded police station, when the policewoman entered.

Immediately, on recognising her from the training course, the inspector enquired across the crowded office, 'How's your head, Angela?'

To which the policewoman shouted back, 'Well, I've never had any complaints so far!'

Wee Polis

...

One evening the police received an urgent call for assistance from an elderly woman who sounded distressed.

The police officers, led by the new shift inspector, immediately made their way out of the station to the location.

On arrival, they knocked on the door of the house and a female voice asked from inside, 'Who is it?'

'It's the police!' replied the inspector.

'Who?' responded the elderly woman.

'It's the police, m'dear,' he replied. 'Can you open the door and let us in?'

'How do I know you're the polis?' she enquired.

'I can assure you, m'dear, I am the police!' the inspector said.

'Is that right? Well, how do I know?' said the woman in response.

'Well,' said the inspector, beginning to lose his patience, 'you could look through your letter box and you'll see I'm a police officer!'

At that, the inspector, who was 6 foot 2 inches tall, knelt down on the landing and opened the elderly lady's letter box for her to see out.

The woman looked at the police officer's face, looking back at her.

The inspector then pointed to his police cap badge and the braiding on his hat and said, 'See, I told you I'm the police!'

The woman stared at him for a moment, then responded, 'Away you tae hell! You're too wee for a polis!'

BA with Honours

• • •

A young career-minded police officer was selected to participate on the force's accelerated promotion scheme to become a sergeant.

He was informed he would be moved around the various offices and departments for experience.

First, he was sent to work at the divisional headquarters for a few weeks.

On his first day he was instructed by the senior sergeant to make his way around the entire headquarters building and perform an inventory on how many fire extinguishers there were and their exact locations.

The young sergeant, slightly bemused by this request, said, 'With all due respect, Sergeant, do you mean to tell me that I studied five years at Caledonian University to attain a BA with Honours in order that my first assignment as a newly promoted sergeant would be to try and find my way around an office, which I've never worked in before, and note down how many fire extinguishers there are and their exact location?'

The senior sergeant looked at him and said, 'What did you get the degree for?'

'Geography!' replied the young sergeant indignantly.

'Good!' said the senior sergeant. 'You won't get lost then, will you?'

Drugs Trial

· · ·

At a recent drug-dealer trial in the High Court in Glasgow, a uniformed police officer was explaining to the assembled jury why he had been involved in the raid with undercover Drug Squad officers and his role in the subsequent search of the suspect's property.

As a result of his actions, a large amount of drugs had been recovered and three people arrested and charged in connection with the offence.

The defence QC for the main accused asked the police officer to explain again his part in the operation and subsequent search for drugs.

The officer stated that, on gaining entry to the house, along with the Drug Squad officers, he had begun a meticulous search, one room at a time.

It was whilst engaged in this search that he observed the main accused acting very suspiciously while sitting on one of the beds in the room.

The officer stated that he had moved the accused off the bed and lifted the mattress, to reveal a bag containing a quantity of drugs!

At this point the defence QC interrupted and asked, 'How did you know it was drugs in the bag?'

The officer replied, 'It was a clear plastic bag and I could see the drugs inside. They were in tablet form!'

The defence QC then said, 'So you could tell immediately they were drugs – is that right?'

'Yes, sir, I could,' replied the officer.

The defence QC then said, 'I would like you to answer "yes" or "no" to the following questions I am about to ask you.'

He then picked up a clipboard and pen from his table and asked the officer, 'Are you a chemist?'

'No!' replied the officer.

The defence QC appeared to write something down on the clipboard, before continuing, 'Are you a pharmacist?'

'No!' repeated the officer.

The QC appeared to write down something again. 'Are you an alchemist?'

'No!' replied the officer for a third time.

'Well,' continued the defence QC, 'could you please explain to the ladies and gentlemen of the jury how you can stand there and say that you knew they were drugs just by looking at them?' He then raised his eyebrows, cocked his head to one side and stared at the police officer, inviting an answer.

The officer paused for a moment, as if to give his experienced questioner a ray of hope.

He then rapped his knuckle off the wooden witness podium and said, 'Same as I can tell you this is made of wood, but I'm not a joiner!!'

Suffice to say the jury fell about laughing and the defence had lost a vital point!

Budgie Airways

• • •

When I was a member of Strathclyde Police Motorcycle Section, there was an older officer who claimed to have been a veteran of the RAF.

I would continually rib him and wind him up, and refer to the RAF as being Rude, Arrogant and Fly.

One particular day, we were in the motorcycle section canteen having our lunch and I was deliberately ribbing Old Harry, as usual.

'Come on, Harry, tell everybody what aircraft you have flown yourself. Just you!' I asked sarcastically, then continued, 'The Concorde? A Boeing 747? Or maybe the Starship *Enterprise?*'

As quick as a flash, with his droll, dry sense of humour, Harry replied, 'UFO.'

To this day, I'm not sure if he was just exaggerating or telling me where to go!!

Moody bugger!

The Adventures of Harry the Polis

On the Buses!

...

Several years ago, whilst I was still a serving police officer, my younger brother Hughie was a Corporation Passenger Transport driver.

In layman's terms, he drove a big orange and green double-decker bus about the housing schemes of Glasgow, picking up and dropping off passengers.

It was the practice of all drivers employed on the buses to save money throughout the year and hold a special sports night competition, with free alcohol and buffet for all involved.

They would hire a local social club and make the necessary arrangements for their free night of entertainment with monetary rewards, along with trophies for the winners.

Through Hughie I got to know a lot of the drivers and on these special occasions I would receive an invitation to come along and join in.

It was seven on the Friday night when Hughie arrived in a taxi to pick me up.

He was wearing a white suit and T-shirt to match, in total contrast to my black suit and black T-shirt, so that I appeared like a photographic negative of him.

'Change your suit, Hughie?' I asked him.

'No way,' he said. 'I look like Bryan Ferry in this suit.'

'I don't know about Bryan, but you definitely look like a fairy, that's for sure,' I remarked.

Anyway, Hughie was not for changing his new look, so off we went on our sports night out looking like the new *Randall and Hopkirk (Deceased)*!

On our arrival, the committee members who ran the

event would hand out raffle tickets, five at a time, to the assembled drivers.

Each raffle ticket handed over at the bar was the equivalent of one drink – therefore five raffle tickets equalled five pints of heavy, lager, or any spirit you cared to order.

As the committee member carried out the distribution of tickets at fifteen-minute intervals, he would say to me, 'Sorry, Harry, but Hughie will have to share his drink raffle tickets with you!'

Then, as he was about to move away, he would turn back and, as subtle as a brick to the back of the head, he would press ten raffle tickets into my hand.

This would annoy Hughie: 'How come he gave you more drink tickets than me?'

'What's the difference?' I said. 'We're both going to drink them.'

'Aye, right enough. I'll go and get them in. Is it rum and coke for sir with a beer chaser, or are you on the whisky tonight?'

'One thinks one will enjoy the company and hospitality of one's favourite double act, Mr Whyte and Mr Mackay, thank you very much!'

Off Hughie went to join the queue at the bar, armed with our first supply of drink tickets.

Suddenly a voice rang out across the room. It was Tommy. 'Are you entering any of the competitions, Harry?'

'I might as well,' I replied. 'Put me down for the dominoes and pool. I've trained all week for this.'

'What about the synchronised swimming event?' he joked.

'Oh, I think I'll give it a miss tonight, Tommy – my bikini top has a rip in it anyway,' I replied.

During the events of that evening, I was beaten at the dominoes – that bloody double six beat me every time.

Anyway, I was waiting to take part in the pool games.

Whilst I sat there, draining every drop of the amber liquid from my refillable glass, with my brother Hughie seated alongside me, there appeared a greasy long-haired man, wearing a bright blue jacket with the sleeves rolled up to the elbow in order to reveal several pieces of what appeared to be barbed wire, wrapped ever so ridiculously around his forearm.

To crown it off was a large brass crucifix dangling around his neck, that heavy I would reckon within six months he would resemble the Hunchback of Notre Dame.

He sat down in the chair beside me and said, 'So are you on the buses too?'

'No,' I replied.

'Oh, right,' he said, nodding his head. 'What do you work at, then?'

'I'm a lorry driver,' I responded.

His eyes opened wider. 'A lorry driver? I've always wanted to be a lorry driver. What kind of lorries do you drive then?' he enquired.

'A Scania 110,' I answered.

'A Scania 110? That's my favourite lorry of all time. How long is it and how many wheels does it have?'

Now, at this point, I'm thinking this guy is just out for the day. Where's his psychiatric nurse?

He was obviously a lump of wood in an earlier life!

I turned to Hughie and, on seeing my facial expression change, he got up from his seat and walked over to another bus-driver friend and said, 'Here, Archie, yer mental brother is annoying oor Harry, so ye better have a word with him and tell him to do a drum roll and beat it.'

As Hughie returned to his seat on the opposite side of me, Archie signalled to his brother to come over and said, 'See that bloke ye're talking tae? He's a polis, so don't annoy him, awright?'

Conversation finished, Archie's brother came back over and sat down next to me. He then composed himself and looked both ways and behind himself before staring me right in the face. He then winked and whispered in a low voice, out of the side of his mouth, 'I always wanted to be a polis!'

At which point, I turned my head around to look at Hughie, who said under his breath, 'Lean your head forward as if to pick up your pint and I'll just hook him.'

As it turned out, he was quite a nice lad, although slightly demented.

Also, apart from the barbed wire wrapped around his arms, posing as some sort of modern jewellery, he had a set of car-battery jump leads tied in a neat knot around his neck like a fashion statement.

'Why the jump leads around your neck?' I asked him.

'I forgot that you needed to wear a tie tonight and these were all I could find in the boot of the car!' he replied.

'Awright!' I said. 'Well, you better not "start" anything in here!'

Hughie then spotted the buffet being uncovered on the display tables by Big Andy Hunter. Nicknamed 'Billy Bunter', he was enormous and rumour had it that he was originally a triplet but he ate the other two.

When he was at school, his favourite instrument was the dinner bell.

Hughie moved swiftly to the front of the queue and shouted over to me, 'Harry! Do you want toad in the hole wi' some salad?'

'If you don't mind, Hughie,' I responded, 'I'll just have the salad. I've been toed in the arse once and didn't really enjoy it.'

The assembled queue of drunken bus drivers laughed in unison.

Much later, after the buffet was cleared away and many, many more whiskies were consumed by yours truly, I was summoned to the pool table to play my first game.

'Right, Harry,' said the organiser, 'you're on this side with the rest of the OMOs here.'

'Ho!' I said, taking great exception to this remark, then Hughie explained what he meant by 'OMO'. It was One-Man-Operated bus drivers and not 'homo' as in a sexual preference.

Surprisingly, with Hughie's coaching skills, I won the first game very easily. My next couple of games went the same way, as I was finding it all so easy.

The balls, as they say, were running kindly for me and were never too far from a pocket to pot them into.

I was playing like Stephen Hendry – minus his plooks – and, before I knew it, hey, I was in the semi-final of the tournament. I found it very hard to believe because I could hardly see the pool table – never mind the coloured balls.

My opponent broke off and I was bent down, lining up my cue for my first pot at a ball.

'Hold it, Harry!' Hughie said. 'Pot this one first!'

I looked over to see one of my balls covering a pocket and just perfect for potting.

'I never noticed that one – thanks, Hughie,' I replied.

The game continued in this vein for several shots – me bending down to line up a pot and Hughie changing my mind by pointing out a much easier pot to take on. I must have drunk more than him!

All the time Hughie was talking one load of utter 'pish' to my opponent, who was having to use all his concentration skills just to understand what Hughie was saying to him.

As for me, I was closing one eye and trying to focus on my cue ball as it appeared to be moving about the table on its own and thinking to myself, I wish that bloody white cue ball would stop moving!

Then, just as I was about to take my shot, I clearly saw a hand lift up one of my balls and place it in front of the pocket.

I straightened up and composed myself because I decided I must be seeing things – balls don't move about by themselves and, even in my rapidly drunken state, I couldn't piss this mot – I mean, I couldn't miss this pot!

Then I realised why I was so good at pool all of a sudden.

My brother Hughie was talking to my opponent and, while distracting him, he was placing my balls over the pockets for me to pot them, as well as 'potting' a few of my balls into his own trouser pockets.

I wondered how some games seemed to be over very quickly . . . I was only potting half my quota of balls, compared to my opponent's full quota.

Being a conscientious police officer with a reputation for being honest and upholding the law, I couldn't handle the fact that I was in the pool final due to the behaviour of my brother Hughie who was blatantly cheating. With this playing on my mind, I did the only honourable thing available to me! No, I didn't own up – are ye daft? I was winning. I just compromised. I told Hughie I didn't want his help in the final because I was good enough to win it on my own.

Suffice to say I didn't win the final and, to rub salt into my wound, I played total crap and was completely whitewashed. Which, in retrospect was probably a fair result for me.

Come to think of it, even when I play sober, I'm total crap.

However, Hughie reckoned I was extremely lucky to get nil! Which was hurtful, because I do have feelings you know!

During the evening, Hughie had also been helping the committee by handing out the drink raffle tickets and helping himself to several sheets for doing it.

He had also arranged with the girl behind the bar to allow us to trade them in for a carry out and had placed an order for a bottle of whisky, a bottle of rum and two dozen cans of Red Stripe lager – just in case we got thirsty on our road home.

I decided we should go for a 'Chic Murray' – an Indian curry – and told Hughie I was going outside for some fresh air, while they were clearing up the tables.

Unfortunately, I forgot to mention to him about going for the curry. While sitting on a wall outside waiting for Hughie, a police panda car pulled up alongside me.

'Hi, Harry!' said the passenger. 'What are you doing here?'

'Oh, hi, Davie!' I replied – it was a friend I had been to college with. I continued, 'I've got this theory, Davie, that the world revolves on an axis so, if I wait here long enough, my house will pass by and I'll get hooked up by the wife!'

'Don't think so, Harry. Why don't you jump in the back and we'll give you a lift?' he said.

'OK, Davie,' I replied, getting into the rear of the car.

'Could you drop me off at the Noor Mahal Indian Restaurant in Shawlands? I feel like a wee Chic Murray afore I go home!'

'No problem, Harry!' replied Davie, and promptly drove me to the restaurant, dropping me off at the front entrance.

As I entered, I was shown to a table for two, as I had told them that my brother Hughie would be joining me.

All I remember after that was the waiter nudging me and saying, 'Excuse me, Harry, but we are wishing to go home now and I don't think your brother is coming!'

I looked around me and the restaurant was empty, apart from the staff still clearing up.

'What time is it, Zaffar?' I asked the manager.

'Very late, Harry – quarter to one in the morning. You have been sleeping for ages!' he replied.

While all this was going on, Hughie had come out of the club looking for me, couldn't find me and organised a small search party of his friends to help him check the nearby golf course just in case I had fallen into a bunker.

Having no success in finding me, he then flagged down a 'fast black' taxi and went to my house, where he informed my wife, 'I've lost him – I've lost Harry. One minute he was there and the next minute, poof, he was gone.'

Mind you, I think 'poof' was the wrong choice of word to describe my disappearance from outside the club.

He continued explaining, 'I've been up and down the golf course next to the club looking for him in case he fell into a bunker! Some of the guys helping to look for him nearly shat themselves and ran off when they saw me dressed in white coming towards them in the darkness!'

All the while, my missus stood with her arms folded, listening to this pathetic tale of woe from my drunken brother, totally unconcerned.

Poor Hughie, he was completely demented and unaware that I was wrapped up, as snug as a bug in a rug, in the spare room of my parents' house, snoring away like the proverbial pig, with my runner-up medal for the pool competition along with a crisp £20 note tucked away in my breast pocket.

Roll on the next games night on the buses!

'Fares, please!'

Canteen Patter

• • •

Big Eddie Oliver, a police motorcyclist, called at the Force Training Centre canteen.

As he approached the hot plate counter, he asked the assistant, 'Here, Cathy, have you got a plate of yesterday's soup?'

To which Cathy replied, 'Certainly, Eddie. Come back tomorrow!'

German Knockers

...

Several years ago, my partner O'Reilly and I were engaged in motorcycle patrol duties when we were instructed by the duty officer of the division to check all the local schools in our area, due to an ongoing complaint of vandalism.

With this in mind, we went out on our police patrol.

Travelling along a road in Glasgow, I observed two men and a woman loitering outside the gates of a school.

We about-turned and headed back down towards the school, whereby one of the men, who was wearing a black cowboy hat, had climbed over the metal railings into the school and, along with the other man, was attempting to assist the young woman, who was wearing a black miniskirt and a bikini-style T-shirt, barely covering her rather large bust and revealing a very bronzed midriff.

As we pulled up alongside them, I enquired what they were doing in the school grounds.

One of the men answered in a broken English accent, 'Vee are German students and vee stay in zee school, yah?'

'Oh, so you're Germans?' I replied.

Then as I looked over at the well-endowed girl, I thought I would be smart and said, 'Your wee bird has got some pair of knockers for her size!'

To my complete and utter embarrassment, the girl replied in a broad Glaswegian accent, 'Ho, you! He's bloody German, no' me!!'

Exit very quickly two red-faced police officers!

The Smell of Robbery

...

In the early eighties, due to an increase in armed robberies in the Strathclyde area in particular, the police decided to set up 'Special Anti-Crime Teams' in order to try and combat them.

I was enrolled as a member of this section and our objective was, whenever the police radio operator broadcast a certain code word over the airwaves, followed by the location, we would respond immediately at high speed to the call.

However, this entailed a lot of patience, watching and waiting.

In order to pass the time, I began to make up my own code names for the various teams of police officers involved and came up with the following abbreviations:

FART: which would stand for Fast Action Response Team;

SHIT: which would stand for the CID or the Strathclyde High Intelligence Team, hence the expression, 'The CID, what a load of shit!'

Then I came up with:

CRAP: which would refer to the Criminal Response Action Patrol.

You should by now see the direction in which I was heading, and especially where my ideas were coming from.

Another which readily springs to mind is:

ARSES: they were the Anti-Robbery Squad Enquiries Section.

Finally, the last section I came up with was:

POOFS: who have absolutely nothing to do with the team you're maybe thinking about, or who readily come to mind, but are the Police Operational Order Form Section, who would deal with all new legislation resulting from the enquiries performed by the other crime teams.

They're what we term the 'back-up' team.

So please, don't even whisper under your breath what you think of it, for I'm just as likely to make up another squad from your expression and it's even more likely to be accepted!

Mind you, I should have said, I've just got 'wind' that they're still recognised as 'FARTS' within the police, having recently been informed that the 'FART' team was still the term being used.

Is That Right?

. . .

An ex-cop's son applied for a position in the police as a civilian force station assistant, working in the front office, dealing with members of the public.

After receiving several knockbacks for the post, his father decided to write to the police personnel department for an explanation as to why he was not being considered.

He received a written response a few days later from the head of the personnel department, stating that his son's application had contained far too many 'speeling' mistakes.

Speeding Excuses

· · ·

The speed radar unit stopped a car for exceeding the limit.

As they spoke with the male driver and made him aware of the offence, his passenger wife insisted in interrupting the police officers at every opportunity, saying how surprised she was that her husband should be stopped for speeding rather than her:

'I can't believe he has been caught breaking the speed limit, because he is a funeral director and is used to driving slowly. Now if it had been me driving, I could understand it, because I'm always speeding about in the car!'

The reporting officer then interrupted her and said, 'Well, if you'd like to wait until I'm finished with your husband, I'll be delighted to take down your full confession in writing!'

That's Entertainment

· · ·

A few years ago, when I performed with a Scottish folk band, we were playing a concert at a local theatre.

During the performance a fight broke out at the rear of the hall and a bottle was thrown from the back, which struck a man in the front row on the head.

Concerned for the man and the injury to his head and having been trained in first aid as a police officer, I jumped off-stage to tend his injury.

'Are you all right, mate, are you all right?' I enquired.

Without looking, the man quickly replied, 'Naw, I'm not! Hit me again, I can still hear ye playing!'

Help the Aged

• • •

One day whilst engaged on uniform beat duty, I saw an elderly woman struggling with several heavy grocery bags.

Being a considerate police officer in the community, I went over to her and said, 'Give me your bags, hen, and I'll carry them for you.'

'Oh, thanks, son, that's very kind of you. I'm just up this close here,' she said, pointing to an old tenement building.

I carried them all the way and it was just my luck, she lived in a 'tap dancer'.

Up I went, carrying her bags all the way to the top floor.

When I got to her door, she thanked me very much and said, 'That was awfy good o' you, son. Would you like a nice juicy Jaffa orange?'

'No, thank you, missus,' I politely replied.

'Well,' she said, 'whit aboot a wee hauf?'

I thought for a moment, then answered, 'You know, hen, I would love a wee hauf!'

To which she responded, 'Right, then, you hold on to it while I go and get a knife!'

Another Vacancy

• • •

An advertisement for a police cell van driver listed the special qualities required:

'Whilst working alongside police officers, you are expected to be of a high physical fitness and prepared to deal with occasional bouts of bad temper and antisocial behaviour.'

They forgot to clarify to whom this paragraph referred!!

Don't Call Me a Liar

...

One time in the witness box of the Sheriff Court, I was being cross-examined by a very young, inexperienced defence agent.

During his questioning of me, he said, 'I put it to you, officer, that did not happen and what really happened was . . .' *blah blah blah*. He then began to give the court a completely different version of events.

He then looked at me for a response, so I said, 'Are you calling me a liar?'

Quick as a flash, the presiding sheriff intervened: 'Eh, I don't think Mr Ross is saying that, are you, Mr Ross? You're not calling the police officer a liar. Or are you?'

To which Mr Ross, the defence lawyer, surprised and somewhat flustered by my response to his scenario, said, 'Certainly not, m'lord, I was only giving an alternative version of events to the police officer, but I have no more questions for the witness!'

My unexpected response worked a treat!

Ill Health Retiral

...

I was summoned to the divisional commander's office.

'You want to see me, sir?' I asked.

'Yes, Morris,' he said. 'I'd like you to retire for health reasons!'

'But I'm not ill, sir!' I pleaded my case.

'Maybe not,' he replied, 'but you make me sick!'

Graffiti

• • •

I attended a call from an Asian grocer's shop, regarding a complaint of graffiti being sprayed on his security shutters.

On arrival, I met with an excited Mr Singh, the shop owner, who spoke to me at 60mph. (That's very fast!)

'Woh! Slow down, Mr Singh!' I said. 'Take a breath, man!'

'I am being very sorry, Mr Harry, but I'm also being very angry with these bastards who do this to me,' he replied.

You could say he was not a happy chapatti!

He then led me back outside his shop and pulled down his security shutters, to reveal in bold black writing, a metre high, the letters 'NF'!

'Look, Mr Harry, look what they have done!' he cried.

I looked at it for a moment, then said, 'C'mon, Mr Singh, you're not seriously suggesting that Nick Faldo was here last night, spray-painting graffiti on your security shutters, because I know for a fact he has a stonewall alibi – he was playing golf in America, 'cause I saw him live on the TV last night.'

He looked at me with a puzzled expression and said, 'No, not Nick Faldo, Mr Harry, but National Front bastards!'

I looked straight at him and replied with a wry smile, 'Nick Faldo? National Front? I personally suspect it was Nick Faldo, 'cause that National Front mob aren't clever enough to spell NF, but what do you think yourself, Mr Singh?'

He stood staring at me for a moment, then a smile broke out across his face and he laughed, 'Okay-dokey, Mr Harry. I'll wash it all off!'

As I left him, I said, 'You do that, Mr Singh, and I'll keep my eye on that bugger Nick Faldo, just in case he comes back here tonight, OK?'

Paton's Place

...

While a guest at Stuart Paton's family party, I noticed a relative of his going to the kitchen several times and returning each time with a glass of lager and a glass of whisky.

I also observed that he did not appear any worse for the amount of alcohol he was drinking.

The next time he returned from the kitchen with a replenished 'glass' in hand, I remarked for all to hear, 'Hey, big man, you certainly like your bevvy, I think you must have hollow legs. If I drank as much as you, I'd be legless!'

There was silence for a moment, before the assembled party of guests burst into hysterical laughter.

What was funny about that, then? I thought to myself.

Then Stuart informed me that his relative, 'oor Tam', had an artificial leg!

Talk about putting your foot in it!

However, as if that wasn't bad enough, I later told a joke about leaving for school one morning and when I returned home, my family had moved house to a different area of Glasgow without telling me.

Again there was silence, followed by hysterical laughter.

It transpired that one of the women at the party had suffered that very same scenario that I had related in my joke, and to crown it all off, she just happened to be married to 'oor Tam', the guy with the artificial leg.

There's nothing like keeping it in the family, I suppose!

TV Detectives

. . .

One particular night shift, about half past one in the morning, I was walking 'the beat' along the Cathcart Road in Glasgow with my partner Joe Doris when we were stopped by a taxi driver who informed us he had picked up a man, carrying a large 26-inch television set, from the Langside area and dropped him off at a tenement building in Govanhill.

We both agreed this was a suspicious circumstance indeed.

The taxi driver took us down to where he had dropped the man off and pointed to the building he had entered with the television.

He also provided us with a full description of our suspect.

We entered the tenement close and listened outside the main door of each apartment.

We performed this procedure at three doors, when bingo, at the fourth door we could distinctly hear a man and a woman talking. The woman was saying, 'Don't leave the auld wan there, I'll fall o'er it during the night when I get up for a pee!'

Could this be a television she was referring to? Well, we thought so.

They sounded like they were in the hallway, close to the front door.

I knocked on the door and immediately heard the man say, 'Don't answer it, let's just keep quiet!'

I knocked on the door again and said, 'Can you open the door, please? It's the police. We know you're in there, we can hear you both talking!'

Next thing I heard was something being dragged towards the rear of the door.

'Open the door or I'll force it!' I said with a voice of authority.

By this time, Joe had gone to the back of the tenement building and climbed up to the rear window, where he saw the man dragging a set of bedroom drawers into the hallway, obviously to barricade the front door and prevent us from gaining entry.

I informed the suspect that we knew what he was doing and advised him to open the door voluntarily, or we would have to use force to gain entry.

'Just hawd yer hoarses!' the woman shouted. I then heard her saying to the man, 'Open the bloody door, Sammy. I don't want it kicked in wi' them bastards, they sound a bit gung-ho tae me!'

Moments later the door was opened and inside, in full view, was the suspect stolen television, occupying pride of place on the wooden sideboard in the living room area.

Several questions later, the male suspect was still vehemently denying having stolen it.

Then the wife said, in typical 'Glesca' fashion, 'Aw, fur fuxsakes, Sammy, tell 'em where ye blagged it, afore they empty the bloody hoose intae the street and dae us for no' havin' a TV licence as well!'

He then relented and told us he had stolen it from the bar lounge of a well-known Southside hotel.

Apparently, as he waited outside, the window of the TV lounge area was opened and several spent cigarettes were discarded on to the lawn.

An hour or so later the residents, who were all drinking, eventually retired to their rooms for the night, leaving the window open.

He then climbed inside the open window and promptly

removed the television from a wall shelf.

As a footnote, the hotel residents who were drinking and to whom he referred in his admission just happened to be nine CID detective police officers, who were staying at the hotel while attending a detectives' course at the Police Training School in Glasgow!

Oops! Not exactly the best of starts to their detection course – maybe a revision course on crime prevention was required!

The Glasgow Sheriff Court

...

There was a particularly well-known sheriff in Glasgow who was renowned for his hard line on what may be described as 'the neds'!

One day he entered his court, which was crowded with lawyers and the general public.

As he surveyed the court, his attention was drawn to a scruffy young male at the rear who did not stand to attention like everyone else when the sheriff had entered.

Instead, the insolent young ned continued to lounge in his seat, with his hands thrust in his pockets, chewing loudly on a piece of gum.

The angry sheriff summoned his court usher and said, 'Kindly inform that young man at the rear that I will not tolerate mastication in my court!'

The bemused and more than confused usher walked back up the court to the youth and said firmly, 'Right you! The sheriff says you've tae get yer hauns oot yer poackets, ya dirty wee bugger!'

The Sheehy Report

· · ·

Several years ago the police force was to undergo radical changes as far as the serving members were concerned, with the arrival of Sir Patrick Sheehy and his proposed Sheehy Report for the police.

The Police Federation, who represent force members, held what was commonly referred to as a Greeting Meeting, in order to discuss some of the aspects of the forthcoming report.

During the meeting, questions were asked and unsatisfactory answers given.

One of the police officers nearest the front of the hall, who was totally disillusioned by all that had gone before, stood up and said, 'Correct me if I'm wrong, but I believe the Sheehy Report implements many changes to the police force as we all know it?'

'That is correct,' replied the Federation representative.

'Well!' continued the officer. 'I'm convinced that all these sweeping changes have already taken place and you, as our Federation, representing the rank and file, have not opposed a single point. In fact, I would go as far as to say all you have done is dilute them!'

He then paused for a moment, before continuing, 'Allow me to provide you with an example of how I see it!'

'It appears to me that if the Sheehy Report had said, "All serving members of the police force will stand with their heads in a bucket of shite for ten minutes every shift," you, the Federation, would have considered it a victory if you had it reduced to five minutes per shift!!'

The Tasmanian Devil

• • •

During the World Pipe Band Championships at Bellahouston Park in Glasgow, I was engaged in motor-cycle patrol duties in the park when a young man, dressed in full Highland regalia, tartan kilt and all, approached my partner John Knox and myself and explained that he was a serving police officer from Tasmania, visiting Scotland to take part in the championship.

He asked if he could take a photograph of John and I on our police motorcycles, to which we readily agreed.

He then began to set up his camera, using a light meter and changing the lens and filter.

While he did all this, I interrupted him and suggested he take his photograph from the opposite side, whereby he would also include all the competing pipe bands in the back-ground with their variety of coloured tartans on display.

'Great idea!' he said.

He then proceeded to check the lighting again, changing the camera lens and filters for the new angle I had suggested.

Satisfied he had the correct lighting filters fitted, he began to focus his camera on us.

He then knelt down on the grass to capture his prized photograph, when – bonk! – in true commando-style Scottish-kilt-wearing, I witnessed a most unexpected surprise, as down from below his kilt and on to the grass below dropped his rather well-endowed penis!

This was definitely a 100-per-cent-genuine Tasmanian Devil!

If I didn't know better, I'd have sworn it was eating the grass!

As it was, it certainly appeared to be eating something!

At this point, two elderly women were passing and one of them took an interest in what was happening with us.

On seeing the aforementioned exposed 'Tasmanian Devil' in full view and full colour, she grabbed hold of her friend's arm and in the loudest whisper I've ever heard, she said, 'Peggy! Peggy! Quick! Would you look at the size o' that big beauty, is that no' a monster?'

Peggy turned around and looked on in amazement, then said to the young photographer, 'I bet you're not from around here, son?'

'No, ma'am,' he replied in a proud voice. 'I'm from Tasmania!'

'Of course you are and you're obviously eating the right things 'cause you're a fine specimen of a boy!' Peggy said.

'Why thank you, ma'am!' he said, happily blushing.

'By the way!' Peggy added, 'you almost gave Cathy a stroke!'

'No, he did not!' interrupted Cathy, then in a wicked girly voice she said, 'But I wish he would have!'

Both women then walked off giggling like a pair of naughty young schoolgirls.

As for our Tasmanian police colleague, he was none the wiser as to what he had done, or the unexpected thrill he had bestowed upon two elderly Glasgow spinsters on a day out, strolling in the park!

I often wonder, thinking back to that day, if that is why all photographers use the saying, 'Watch the birdie!'

Legless in Auchterarder

· · ·

Whilst attending the Police Convalescent Home in Auchterarder, Scotland, I met up with a remarkable police officer from the Royal Ulster Constabulary in Northern Ireland called Billy!

Billy had tragically lost his right arm from above the elbow and his left leg from above the knee, during a terrorist bomb explosion while on his police patrol.

Despite the loss of his limbs, coupled with the obvious pain and discomfort he endured wearing artificial limbs, Billy showed a wonderful outlook in life and had an amazing sense of humour.

One night, during our time together at the home, Billy and I had gone out for a few drinks.

However, a few became several, as we relaxed in the local hotel lounge, exchanging funny jokes and stories.

Before we knew it, the bar lounge was closing.

I decided to have one more drink for the road, while Billy went off to the toilet.

As I sat there waiting for Billy to return, I realised he was taking quite a long time and with his physical condition, coupled with the amount of drink we had consumed, he may have fallen over.

I went to the toilet to check on him, but to my surprise, there was no sign of Billy.

As I walked out of the hotel, I saw Billy lying flat out on the roadway, trying unsuccessfully to get up.

I ran over to him and said in a concerned voice, 'Billy! Billy, are you OK?'

Billy replied in his broad Irish brogue, 'Of course I'm not OK, Harry, I'm fuckin' legless!'

As both of us began to laugh, I looked over and saw Billy's artificial leg lying on the other side of the road.

Apparently Billy had tried to kick an empty Coke can lying on the footpath and his leg shot off across the roadway!

Football Crazy
· · ·

John Reilly was involved in policing the Old Firm derby at Celtic Park in Glasgow.

This involved him walking around the perimeter track during the game and preventing any hooligans from running on to the field of play, or throwing any objects.

As John walked around, he couldn't avoid watching the game and, being a keen Celtic supporter, he was becoming more and more anxious, as time ticked away and his team chased an equalising goal.

Three minutes to go until full-time and Celtic bundled a goal in from a goalmouth scramble.

As the supporters went wild with excitement, John got caught up in the hype of it all and threw his police hat into the air!

With his arms raised in ecstatic celebration, the swirling wind in the enclosed stadium caught his hat and carried it on to the centre of the field of play, whereby one of the Rangers players retrieved it for him.

The police football commander, having witnessed John's reaction to this goal, made sure John never, ever worked at another football game in which Celtic were involved.

Face Like a Fish Supper . . . All Chips

. . .

I had just left police headquarters, Pitt Street, on my police motorcycle and was riding along the Clydeside Expressway.

I had overtaken several vehicles as I made my way back to the traffic depot.

I was approaching another vehicle in front of me when I noticed it was wavering slightly from side to side, while the driver appeared to be acting very suspiciously.

His head was bobbing up and down and he looked as though he was doing something other than concentrating on his driving!

I decided to pull alongside the driver's window and have a look inside the car for myself.

I was almost at the rear door of the car when the driver's window opened and a newspaper full of chips was discarded out the window, splattering me and my motorcycle!

That was it!

I activated my siren and blue lights and signalled the startled driver to pull over and stop!!

I'm positive I saw him in his rear-view mirror mouth, 'Ohhh, shiiit!'

I got off my motorcycle, dusted myself down of chips and walked towards the car.

The driver gave the impression he would have liked the ground to open up there and then and swallow him and his chips.

However, having a sense of humour, I had to see the funny side. So rather than charge him with an offence, I stopped all the traffic on the Expressway and made him walk back along the carriageway and pick up the newspaper and every chip he had hit me with!

Fortunately for him, I had already eaten the chip that was on my shoulder!

Pieces of Pizza

• • •

From *The Adventures of Harry the Polis*

Harry the Polis walked into a fast food shop and ordered up a pizza.

'It'll be about fifteen minutes!' said the counter assistant.

'That's OK,' replied Harry.

He then waited while the pizza was being cooked in the oven.

When it was ready, the assistant asked Harry, 'Would you like it cut into four or eight pieces?'

Harry replied in all seriousness, 'You'd better cut it into four, hen, I couldn't eat eight pieces!!'

Tulliallan Barbers

• • •

New recruits at Tulliallan Police College have found a way to grow their hair longer, without the instructors noticing.

Apparently they're getting their ears pulled out further!

You Said It!

...

My partner and I called at a Southside motor repair garage to organise a repair to his car.

The garage 'boy' (I use that word loosely), who swept up the floors and ran some errands for the owner, was an old likeable dosser called Jack Barnes, who had a serious drink problem but, unlike many of his drinking buddies, Jack's brain was as sharp as a tack.

'If ye're looking for the boss, he's no' in yet!' Jack greeted us in his usual gruff voice.

'That's OK, Jack, we'll just wait!' I replied.

After a few minutes, we decided to have something to eat, so I said, 'Jack, could you nip around to the greasy spoon and get me two rolls with scrambled egg and two cups of coffee?'

'Aye, nae bother!' said an obliging Jack.

I then handed him over a £10 note and said, 'Get something for yourself, Jack!'

A short time later, Jack arrived back and handed me the coffee and rolls, then pushed the change into my hand.

As I put the coffee and rolls down, I checked my change. 'Ho, Jack, two pound sixty change – where's the rest of my money?'

To which Jack replied in his gruff old voice, 'Ye told me tae get something for mysel', so I bought a half bottle o' wine.'

My partner and I just burst out laughing!

Old Jack Barnes didn't have a scrambled brain, that's for sure!

Housebreaking

• • •

Harry the Polis was late for work one morning and arrived at the office, just as the shift was being detailed their duties by the duty sergeant.

'Sorry I'm late, Sarge, but I came home last night to find my apartment had been tanned!!'

The entire shift was stunned by this news.

'How did it happen?' asked the concerned shift sergeant.

To which Harry replied, 'The wife left her sunbed on all night!'

Reducing Crime

• • •

The chief constable of Strathclyde, working in conjunction with the various regional councils, has devised a plan to help reduce the amount of crime on our streets by 50 per cent.

Apparently they're going to double the number of streets!!

Don't Trust the Polis

• • •

A number of crimes have taken place recently whereby the suspect involved was a bogus police officer.

An alarmed senior officer was prompted to issue a statement to the public, informing them not to trust anyone claiming to be a policeman!!!

The Adventures of Harry the Polis

No Chance

· · ·

Constable Paul was absolutely delighted when he won the tickets for the hospitality suite at Ibrox Stadium to watch his favourites, Glasgow Rangers, play an important league game.

His prize also included a four-course meal, champagne and other refreshments at half-time and full-time.

Excited to get going, he awoke his wife, who was in bed after a busy nightshift, and asked her to drive him to the stadium to drop him off.

Barely awake and wearing her Winnie the Pooh pyjamas, his wife duly obliged.

Afterwards, as she drove back home, she realised, she had no keys to get into the house and about-turned and made her way back to the stadium, where she had to make her way through hundreds of football supporters, to get to the stewards at the front door of the main entrance.

'Excuse me, but I've just dropped my husband off for the game and I haven't any house keys. Could you possibly give him a call over your tannoy and ask him to come to the front door with his house keys?' she asked.

'Certainly, love,' said the steward, and looking at her Winnie top, he added, 'Seeing you're one of the teddy bears. What's his name?'

She paused for a moment before uttering the words, 'It's John Paul!' She then added, 'But I can assure you he's a Rangers supporter!'

The steward looked at her and said, 'Hen! This is Ibrox Park. If I broadcast the name "John Paul" over the tannoy system, he'll get lynched afore he even reaches the stairways!'

'Well what do you suggest I do, then?' she asked. 'I'm locked out!'

'I'd go home, hen, and call the police,' he suggested.

'I am the police and so is my husband John Paul!' she responded. 'Anyway, they'll just boot the door in! I know what they're like,' she added.

'Well, why don't you go home and boot the door in yersel' and claim some overtime?' he replied condescendingly.

As it was, she made her way home and spent the remainder of the day in her pyjamas in her neighbour's house, until finally a drunk but extremely happy John Paul returned from his hospitality day out, totally unaware.

How Did They Know?
• • •

This was in a newspaper years ago.

'A man discovered in a car with his trousers down at his ankles and a woman astride him was arrested today for impersonating a police officer'!!

Toilet Graffiti
• • •

I had to laugh one evening when I entered the police toilet used by suspects brought to the office for interview.

One had written on the wall: 'My mother made me a poof!'

Underneath it, someone else had written: 'If I send her the wool, would she make me one?'

Jacket In!

· · ·

It was the practice while working in the Production Department of the police to note the time, date, locus, crime/offence and a full description of all items worn or involved in incidents, and for this to be lodged by the reporting officer as productions for the court.

At the completion of a court case, where items were produced as evidence, the procurator fiscal's office would issue a 'release notice' in respect of the items retained by the police.

It was then the duty and responsibility of the production officer to notify the owner of the items to call at the police station and collect them within a certain period of time.

This would result in an official recorded-delivery letter being sent to the address of the named person claiming to be their owner.

After a certain length of time and failed attempts to have the owner call and collect the articles, items such as clothing would be destroyed.

On one particular occasion, I was clearing a serious backlog of clothing, where I had a bag for destroying and a bag for a local church charity group, who were collecting warm clothing and blankets for the charity Bosnia Aid.

Any warm or half-decent items of clothing I came across for disposal/destruction, I would put into the Bosnia Aid charity bag!

Several weeks later, having dropped off the black plastic bin bags of clothing at the church, I received a telephone call from a young man requesting the return of his confiscated jacket.

I checked the relevant property book regarding his request, but could find no information as to the whereabouts of this particularly distinctive jacket in his name.

He explained that there were complications in his request, in as much as he was not the person wearing it at the time the police had retained it as a court production.

He then stated that the jacket was being worn by his cousin at the time of the offence, and therefore it would be lodged by the police under this cousin's name.

I then looked under the name and address of his cousin and, sure enough, I found it.

But unfortunately for him and to his utter disappointment, it had not been reclaimed during the retaining period and therefore, as per force instructions regarding unclaimed items, it had been destroyed.

The caller blew his top big-time!

'Destroyed?' he shouted down the telephone. 'Destroyed my arse! You're winding me up, big man!'

'I can assure you, sir, I am not!' I replied. 'The named owner, who according to the records was your cousin, was contacted by Royal Mail recorded delivery several months ago, to contact this office and arrange for the collection of the jacket. He failed to do so within the retention time!'

'But it's my jacket!' he said.

I responded, 'And?' but before I could finish, he interrupted.

'It's a big bloody bright orange North Face jacket, worth over three hundred quid – you couldn't miss it!' he said aggressively.

'Well, I'm sorry, mate, but I would take it up with your cousin and ask him why he didn't call to collect it when he was notified by recorded delivery,' I replied.

'Are you for real, mate?' he enquired. 'You're telling me you've destroyed a three-hundred-quid North Face waterproof, thermal jacket?'

'Not at all, sir. I'm telling you I destroyed a big orange-coloured jacket belonging to your cousin. How much it cost, I don't know. How fashionable it was, I couldn't care less. So I suggest you speak with him about it!' I then replaced the telephone.

However, this entire episode of events prompted an interested response in me.

Thereafter, every night, when I watched the television news or a humane relief documentary, where charity aid workers were involved, I was always conscious of the fact that some poor wee refugee guy was walking about with a 300-quid, bright orange North Face waterproof thermal jacket on, none the wiser of its make, expensive value, or even the fact that it's all the rage in the yuppie fashion scene, but just extremely grateful and delighted to be keeping warm and dry in the freezing cold!

Cruelty to Girlfriends

• • •

Sitting in the police canteen, I was joined by the office cleaner.

As she sat down beside me, I was reading an article from the daily newspaper.

'How disgusting can you get?' I remarked. 'A man's been charged with indecent behaviour towards a nanny goat. Is that no' terrible?'

To which the cleaner replied, 'Not really. Sounds a bit like my son and his new girlfriend!'

The Carbolic Alcoholic

· · ·

As a raw recruit in 1972, I was farmed out to work the Oatlands area, bordering the infamous Gorbals.

I was partnered off with an old cop with several weeks of his police service remaining before he officially retired.

As I was leaving the muster room, after being detailed my duty, another young cop approached me and enquired, 'Are you working with "Soapy", Harry?'

'Soapy?' I said, shaking my head. 'No, it's Davie I'm working with.'

'Soapy,' he said, nodding his head. 'That's his nick-name.'

'How come?' I enquired.

'Just wait. You'll see!' He then laughed and walked off.

Davie had been a real character and a police officer with a great track record.

However, due to the recent death of his wife, Davie had struggled to overcome her loss and found solace in alcohol.

On this particular Sunday afternoon, Davie took me out with him to meet the gatehouse man at a local factory in our area.

I thought we were there for a cup of tea, but Davie and the gatehouse man had other ideas and were pouring and drinking something that was the same colour, but entirely different.

A short time later, we received a call on our personal radios that the shift sergeant and inspector were requesting our locus to rendezvous with us.

Davie answered the radio and began making screeching and burping noises, which didn't make any sense, but sounded like wireless distortion.

He then turned to me, grabbed his hat and coat, then said, 'Quick, Harry, follow me and run like hell!'

We ran halfway down the road, when the radio controller broadcast, 'Would the station trying to transmit please note you have a very poor signal with a lot of interference. I suggest you change your position and try again!'

Further down the road, Davie stopped and transmitted his screeching and burping noises again over his personal radio.

He then looked over at me and, catching his breath, he heaved a huge sigh and said, 'Right, go!'

We were off again down the road until we came to the bottom of Polmadie Road and Old Rutherglen Road, where there was an old-fashioned police box.

(Remember them – *Doctor Who* and all that?)

Davie put his key in the lock and opened the door for us both to enter, he then stood for a moment inside, while he tried to catch his breath, then he put his hand behind the telephone and produced a polythene bag which appeared to contain pieces of tablet.

I watched him as he took a piece of the tablet out of the bag and popped it in his mouth. He began to chew vigorously on it.

The smell emanating from his mouth was revolting and as if that wasn't enough, a yellow bile began to pour profusely out of either side of his mouth, as he continued to chew on the tablet.

'What the hell are you eating, Davie?' I enquired, while screwing my face up in utter disgust at the stench.

'It's carbolic soap, son, guaranteed to mask the smell of the best twelve-year-old Scotch whisky!' he said confidently, while foam still spouted from his mouth like a rabid dog and dripped uncontrollably down his uniform tunic and on to the floor.

'Carbolic soap?' I said. 'Are you serious? You're breath is absolutely bowfin, man, and you look as if you've got rabies!'

'Maybe so,' he said. 'But you can get disciplined for smelling of drink, whereas you can't get done for smelling of soap.'

With that, he tapped the side of his nose with his fore-finger and winked an eye.

'Do you think so?' I replied. 'Well, you should get done for just being totally mingin'!'

Just at that point, we could see the supervisors approaching us.

Davie put his bag of soap tablets back behind the tele-phone, emptied his mouth of foaming spittle and wiped his lips with the sleeve of his tunic, before leaving the police box to greet them.

It took me all my time not to laugh, as Davie conversed with the gaffers, unaware he was still slobbering bile at the mouth.

As for the gaffers, they were just desperate to get away.

I learned a big lesson that day: never drink on duty and you won't have to wash your mouth out with carbolic like Soapy, and also pay particular attention to the nicknames of your partners – as Lloyd Grossman would say, the clues are there!

Such as Gattling Gub (talks non-stop), Olympic Flame (never goes out), Sergeant Signal (the tube with the stripes), the Itch (gets right under your skin) and Harpic (he was clean round the bend)!

The following day, I was partnered off with Big Dick Bruce!!

I'm Sick, Sick, Sick up to Here!
. . .

I followed a car that was being driven in excess of the 30mph speed limit, down a particularly busy accident blackspot road.

Having covered the required measured distance, I activated the blue lights and siren to signal the woman driver to pull over and stop.

Once stopped, I walked up to the driver's door.

The driver was sitting inside, staring directly ahead.

I asked her to open the window but she ignored my request.

I then opened her door myself and, as I did, she vomited all over her steering wheel and dashboard.

She was so worked up and nervous at being stopped by the police, she made herself so physically sick and couldn't stop spewing all over her car.

Therefore, I used my discretion and reckoned if I didn't make a hasty retreat, she would be spewing all over me as well.

Having witnessed her obvious distress, I decided under the circumstances that a warning would suffice and allowed her to carry on her way!

By the way, she was also totally mingin' wi' the vomit!

Michael Schumacher . . . Not!

...

One early morning I attended a call, along with other police mobile stations, to the Old King George V Dock in Govan.

My partner, Graeme Povey, had been putting up a case for our Ford Consul GT being faster than George Dalglish and David Ball's new Jaguar 4.2-litre.

George had baited Povey that he would leave him trailing in his wake if they both had to race to an emergency, since he had a 4.2-litre Jag.

The inevitable was decided: we would have a race along the old derelict dock roads to see which car was the fastest.

We lined up alongside each other, then — go! – we were off, hurtling along the cobbled dock roads at great speed.

Graeme managed to edge our car in front as we approached the winning post.

I looked back with great relief and delight that my underwear was still unsoiled and was about to wave bye-bye to George and David, only to see them juddering to a sudden stop as smoke appeared from the engine of the Jag.

What could have happened, I hear you ask?

Did they blow up the engine? . . . No!

The Jaguar has considerably less ground clearance than most cars and as a result, while hurtling along, George had straddled a metal stud which just happened to be the remains of a capstan (not the cigarette)!

Whereby the engine cross-member of the Jaguar was caught by the protruding stud and virtually removed the whole engine, as the momentum of the bodywork went forward, causing considerable extensive damage to the Jag.

This was an incident that required some expert story-telling from the 4.2 Jaguar car crew!

Vasectomy

. . .

Several years ago, having made the decision not to have any more children, I reluctantly agreed to go for a vasectomy operation, although I was slightly apprehensive about it.

The doctor tried to allay my fears by saying, 'A wee snip here and a wee snip there and Bob's your auntie! So to speak!'

'You're supposed to instil a bit of confidence, doctor!'

However, my sinister-in-law (that's what I call her) added her tuppence worth to my concerns, just to make me feel better: 'It's a dawdle for a man. You don't feel a thing!' she stated.

I responded by saying, 'Is that right? And you would know from experience, I expect, having been a man in an earlier life!'

You'll have guessed I don't get on with her! (Him!!)

Moustache You a Question

• • •

While serving my police probation period at the Gorbals police station, I turned up for the first night of my five weeks' nightshift, sporting a rather faint but visible 'Pancho Villa' Mexican moustache.

The guys had informed me on my shift that if you want to grow a moustache, you either do it on your annual leave or during the nightshift.

This was the present trend of style of facial hair and I must admit, I thought I looked darn well cool for cats, so to speak!

I sat in the muster room along with the rest of my police colleagues, awaiting my duty detail, stroking my face like a veteran moustache-grower and making sure I drew attention to it, just in case someone present hadn't noticed.

There were the usual remarks: 'Something up with your lip, Harry?' 'Could you no' wash yer face afore you came out to yer work, son?'

At the end of the rib-taking and muster, I was summoned to Inspector Wilson's office.

I knocked on his door and was instructed to enter.

As I did, I was asked the following: 'What is that on your face, Harry?'

'It's a moustache I'm growing, sir!' I replied, rather pleased with myself.

'A moustache?' he said. 'Well, take that, Harry!'

He then handed me a blue form.

In all my innocence, I thought I had to fill it out in order to state my intention and obtain permission to grow my moustache.

'What's it for, sir, permission to grow it?' I asked.

'No!' he replied. 'It's a resignation form. If you think you suit the moustache, fill it in and hand it back to me!'

– Baldy old bastard!

Pea and Ham from a Chicken
• • •

My sister Linda invited me over for a barbecue one summer's day and I volunteered to do the cooking.

I was making chicken drumsticks, sausages, burgers and pork chops.

After I had finished cooking, Gary, my sister's young son, helped himself to a large pork chop and went out to the front of his house, where he joined my daughter and his friends.

'Whit's that you're eating, Gary?' asked one of his pals.

'It's a pork chop!' he replied smugly.

'Where did you get it from?' asked another friend.

Gary replied sarcastically, 'From a cow, stupid!'

At which point, my youngest daughter Kimmy said, 'No, Gary, it's from a pig . . . Stupid!'

The Snitch
• • •

It is common knowledge amongst the rank and file that a well-known senior police officer got a young policewoman into trouble.

Apparently he reported to a traffic warden she was parked on a double yellow line!

Taxi to Charing Cross

•••

While performing surveillance duties with the Serious Crime Squad, I was following a car being driven by the target male along a busy road in Glasgow city centre.

At this time, I was driving a black taxi, which we used from time to time, and I was the tail end in the surveillance team operating that day.

I was instructed by radio to close in on the target and take over the main role, while the lead vehicle was replaced to avoid any suspicion by the suspect.

As I moved up through the traffic on the target vehicle, I was stopped in a line of vehicles at traffic lights.

While waiting for the lights to change, I was watching the target vehicle closely for any sudden movements from him, when suddenly the door of my taxi opened and a well-dressed, suited man got into the back seat.

'Charing Cross please, driver,' he said.

I turned around to look at him and said politely, 'Sorry, mate, I'm not for hire!'

'Well your light's on, so you'll have to take me,' he replied.

I looked over to see the opposite junction traffic lights change to red and turned back to my passenger.

'Right, mate, you'll have to get out,' I said. 'I'm busy!'

'I beg your pardon?' he enquired.

'You heard me, I'm busy, now get out the taxi!' I repeated.

'You're for hire and I'm hiring you to drive me to Charing Cross!' he replied rather indignantly.

'And I'm telling you to sling yer hook and get out my taxi,' I responded in a stern voice. 'Now move yer arse and hurry up about it!'

'That's it! You've gone too far, now I'm going to report you!' he responded in true Basil Fawlty fashion.

Then, taking a notebook and pen from his breast pocket, he began scribbling notes down in it.

By this time, the traffic was starting to move off and I was instructed over my police radio, 'Right, Harry, move up, move up, the target is now yours!'

Now I was getting really annoyed, so I said to my passenger, 'Right, mate, write this down: "I am personally going to batter you if you don't get out my taxi right now." Comprendez?'

'That's it, so you're threatening me with violence? You are in such deep trouble, my man! They'll throw the book at you!' he replied, while writing in his wee notebook.

Then, blasting loudly over my police radio came: 'Harry, what is keeping you? Will you move up on the target before the traffic lights change again!'

This was the final straw — my patience was exhausted, so I opened my driver's door.

'That's it, pal, you've had your chance!' I said.

I jumped out of the driving seat, opened the passenger door and, grabbing hold of his jacket collar, I physically pulled him out of his seat.

At this point, he wrapped his arms around the passenger handlebar rail and held on tightly, refusing to budge.

'I'll call the police on you!' he said, clinging on like a leech.

'Don't bother, I'm here!' I said. 'Now do yerself a Rodney and piss off!'

I then threw his briefcase and brolly out on to the pavement before he would move.

I got back into the taxi and drove off into the lead position, where I continued with my surveillance of the target vehicle.

However, as I looked back, I saw my evicted passenger flag down another taxi and get in.

I had to laugh when I thought of the taxi driver asking him, 'Where to, mate?'

And him replying, 'Follow that cab!!'

Exam Results

• • •

During the Police Scotland Examinations, an officer was taken aside by the adjudication officer and informed he was being reported to the Examination Board for cheating.

'Who, me?' said the surprised officer. 'Where did I cheat then?'

The examiner replied, 'Question eight!'

'What about question eight?' asked the officer.

'Well,' said the adjudicator, 'the person sitting on your immediate right has written his answer as, "I don't know"! And you've written, "I don't know either"!!'

Police Proverb

• • •

My kids handed me a key ring one Christmas, which said, 'Help your local policeman – beat yourself up!!'

Kicking the Habit

· · ·

A man was arrested and, on being searched, was found to be concealing drugs in his training shoes.

When asked to explain his possession of the drugs, he gave the following excuse to the officers, 'I'm genuinely trying to kick the habit!'

Cosmetic Surgery

· · ·

An older female station assistant decided to go for some facial cosmetic surgery. She was not one bit vain about it either and didn't care who knew!

Several months later I happened to be in the office where she worked and on seeing her, I noticed a big difference in her facial appearance. I decided to joke with her:

'Do yer toes always curl up when ye talk?'

'Did ye get everything stretched and lifted?'

'Yer eyes are open awfully wide, Cathy. Can ye no' shut them?'

'Is that a dimple on yer chin or yer belly button?'

She laughed at these but soon got fed up with my constant joking, and pointed her elbow at me and said with a straight face, 'One more remark like that and I'll pish all over you!'

There was a silence, before she burst into hysterical laughter.

Talking Sex

. . .

A black policeman I worked with was employed with the Support Unit, which consisted of a van with usually eight or ten officers who would be deployed into a troublesome area.

One evening an officer nicknamed Gattling Gub was berating him in the van in front of the other officers and making him the butt of his jokes and remarks.

Later that evening, half of them were dropped off at my office for their refreshment period.

As they all sat around the table, enjoying a cigarette and a cup of coffee, one of the officers said to the black officer, 'Why did you put up with that tosser Gattling Gub slagging you off like that? Why did you not just tell him to shut the fuck up?'

The black officer, totally calm and sitting quietly, looking down at his coffee, replied, 'Because, at the end of the day, I know something he doesn't!'

He then paused for a moment before continuing, 'When his wife worked as a cop with me, I had sex with her many times, before him!'

You could hear a pin drop at this remark, then, as one, the entire table of seated cops burst into hysterical laughter!

A Special Unit Burns Supper

. . .

Several years ago, while working in the Crime Intelligence Unit at police headquarters, Pitt Street in Glasgow, I attended a Burns Supper evening of entertainment in the HQ restaurant.

There were some excellent speakers at this well-attended venue and the top table was littered with senior police officers and distinguished guests.

The main guest speaker was a high-profile and colourful character who was a former Conservative MP and highly respected Queen's Counsel.

The start was delayed due to the late arrival of our distinguished guest speaker, who was absolutely pished as a fart on his arrival and decked out in his usual tartan three-piece suit and cravat.

The senior officers and other invited guests squirmed in their seats at his noisy, over-the-top entrance, whereby some of them had to assist him as he staggered unsteadily on his feet.

After a brief slurred apology, which I struggled to make any sense of, it was his big moment to address the haggis!

The chef, carrying the haggis, was led in by a tartan-clad bagpiper and made his way along the front of the top table, stopping directly opposite the guest speaker and placing the impressively large haggis in front of him.

Drams of malt whisky were then handed around the guests before the main speaker began his most notable and totally unforgettable address to the haggis!

He began, 'As a former well-known Barlinnie Special Unit client of mine once said . . .' Pausing for a moment to compose himself, he then blurted out loudly, 'Take that, ya bastard!'

He then began stabbing and thrashing the large butcher knife into the cooked haggis in front of him.

Pieces of haggis were strewn everywhere, all over the top table.

The expressions on the faces of senior officers along the top table were priceless.

As for the assembly seated before them, of which I was one, we howled with laughter at his antics.

However, a few minutes later, it was a case of, 'Taxi for Pitt Street!' as he was whisked off, out of the building, into the night!

Karaoke? Not!

• • •

A police officer, aptly nicknamed 'the Slug' because he was so slow at everything he attempted, was attending the Sheriff Court in Glasgow in order to give evidence at a trial.

While in the witness box, he was being cross-examined by the accused's defence agent.

The officer answered each question that was asked of him, in his own immutable fashion, refusing to allow himself to be harassed or hurried.

This was becoming infuriating to the defence agent, to such an extent that he said abruptly, 'Do you know, Constable, you give the impression of being more laid-back than Perry Como. Would you agree with that statement?'

To which the Slug reacted by shrugging his head from side to side and giving the question some consideration, before replying, 'I'd probably have to agree with you, sir, so long as you don't ask me to sing like him!'

The Adventures of Harry the Polis

CSI Glasgow

...

How do Gil Grissom and his *CSI* team do it, week after week? I mean how do they solve the crimes on TV?

It's one thing to solve it, but it's another thing convincing a jury, particularly a Glasgow jury, to convict an accused on the DNA evidence available.

One particular case comes to mind, whereby an accused, serving a jail term for robbery, attended the High Court in Glasgow for trial on another charge of armed robbery.

During the trial we heard that the accused, along with another male, both wearing ex-USA President Richard Nixon masks, had entered a bank, produced a gun and held up staff and customers, before committing a robbery.

While the bank was being held up, an ex-police officer standing in the queue decided to have a go at the gunman and began to struggle with him, during which he pulled off the gunman's mask, exposing his true identity.

Meanwhile the other robber, with the money, climbed back over the security screen and ran out of the bank and was driven off in a waiting getaway car, leaving the gunman stranded.

The gunman then ran from the bank along the busy main street pursued by the ex-policeman, who shouted out, 'Stop him!'

A male shopper put down the bags he was carrying to intervene, but on seeing the gun in the robber's hand, he stepped out of his way, allowing him to pass unchallenged.

The gunman managed to escape capture at this point, but was later identified and subsequently arrested, along with the gun he used, which was recovered in a shoebox in his house.

Now, the farce referred to as the court case went as follows:

The ex-cop, who had a go with the gunman in the bank and ripped off his Richard Nixon mask, positively identified the accused in the dock as being the person he had fought with and who struck him on the head with the gun, causing injury.

The shopper who had allowed the gunman to pass unobstructed positively identified the accused in the dock as the same person and qualified his evidence by adding, 'When someone is running towards you armed with a handgun, you don't forget what the person looks like!'

Next up were the cops who raided his house and arrested him. During his taped interview with the CID he had freely admitted having bought the Richard Nixon masks worn during the robbery while on a recent weekend trip to Manchester.

Then the final nail in his coffin was the scene-of-crime evidence. Enter the forensic scientist to give his expert evidence. (Yes, just like *CSI*'s Gil Grissom!)

He was the CSI officer who matched the DNA on the hair follicles ripped from the accused's head when he struggled with the ex-cop in the bank and lost his mask.

The forensic officer then gave the odds of one in five million that it wasn't the accused person on trial involved.

In other words, it was the accused male seated in the dock.

The jury went out to deliberate and consider the evidence, before returning a very short time later with a Not Proven verdict!

As for the accused, who expected to be found guilty and sentenced to at least five years, he just burst out laughing at the verdict of a rather weak and totally inept jury.

A Side Order of Vegetables

· · ·

Detective Superintendent Charlie Craig was a very funny guy.

I had been fortunate to hear Charlie as a guest speaker at a function and found him a very witty character.

One time, whilst a guest speaker at a Burns Supper at police HQ in Pitt Street, attended by the deputy and assistant chief constables, Charlie was speaking about the knighthood that had been bestowed upon the present chief constable.

Charlie said that the chief constable had invited his most senior staff members, who just happened to be seated along either side of Charlie at the top table, to accompany him for a meal and a celebration drink.

Once inside the restaurant, the chief constable and his party were escorted to their specially prepared table.

After they were all seated, the waitress noted the drinks order, whilst a second waitress handed out the food menus.

After a few minutes the food menu waitress returned to note each guest's order.

She began with the chief constable.

'Now, sir, what would you like to eat?' she asked politely.

'I'll have the filet mignon, please!' replied the chief constable.

The waitress made note of his order, then asked, 'And what about your vegetables?'

To which he replied, 'Oh, they'll just order for themselves!'

Only 'Cheeky' Charlie would attempt to get away with that one!

Red Card for Pink Slip

• • •

A regular complaint in the police was the number of times members of the public would call at the station to report having lost a bag, a wallet, a handbag or its contents.

At this point I must stress that on most occasions it was usually the loss of a cashed Department of Social Security giro cheque!

With this in mind, they would ask for a pink slip/loss report to present to their insurance company in order to make a claim, but more realistically, if you were on state benefit, you could take it to the DSS office and obtain help with your loss, i.e. a crisis loan, etc.

This procedure was being abused big-time by certain members of the public and was highlighted with a story in the *Sunday Mail* under the heading 'Red Card for Pink Slips', referring to the amount of false reporting!

While I was on duty one Sunday evening, a woman called at the station to report having lost her handbag and asked if I could provide her with a loss report for her insurance company.

Having heard it all before, I handed her a copy of the newspaper and advised her to sit down, read the article and consider the consequences before I processed her request.

I sat back down at my desk and continued with my paperwork.

After a short while, I looked up to see the woman, still peering at the newspaper.

Thinking she might be illiterate, I said, 'Do you have a problem reading the article, missus?'

To which she replied, 'Not normally, sir, but my reading glasses were in my bag when I lost it!'

Ask Him Yourself

...

Out one day on motorcycle duty together with John Imrie, we were patrolling the Great Western Road area of Glasgow when John and I had occasion to stop a van, being driven by a young Asian man, regarding an expired tax disc being displayed.

As the van pulled up outside a mini-market, the young driver got out and went to enter, but was stopped by John.

The driver stated that the van belonged to the shop owner and he was just the delivery driver. He also gave his name as Iqbal Singh.

While John spoke with the driver, I went inside to speak with the shop owner and check the identity of the driver of his van.

I immediately noticed the shop owner was wearing a ring with the name Iqbal on it.

'Can you tell me your name please?' I asked him.

'Iqbal Singh!' he replied. 'I am the shop's owner here!'

'Can you tell me your driver's name?' I enquired.

'As' him!' he replied.

'No, I don't want to ask him, I'm asking you. Now what is his name?' I said with a stern voice, knowing the driver had given a false name to John.

Again, the shopkeeper replied, 'As' him, sir!'

Losing my patience, I replied, 'I told you, I'm asking you, not him! Now tell me his name!'

This time with his voice trembling, he replied, 'As' him, sir, as' him!'

'That's it, this is your final chance to tell me his name,' I said with authority, 'or else I'll charge you with attempting to pervert the course of justice.'

To which the poor frustrated shopkeeper answered, 'As' him, sir! Assim Naseem! Honest!'

Forgot Who You Were Today?

• • •

Whilst patrolling with my partner David Ball, we stopped a vehicle being driven along Edmiston Drive, opposite Ibrox Park in Glasgow.

The driver, who was a young Asian, accompanied us around his car while we examined it for any visible defects.

We asked him to identify himself and to provide some form of proof.

The driver immediately pulled out his wallet and handed over a driving licence bearing the name Abdul Ahmed, and stated that he was the named licence-holder.

While examining it, David noticed that the driver's licence had not been signed by the holder and pointed out that it was an offence.

He handed it back to the driver, along with a pen, to sign it.

The driver took possession of his licence and proceeded to sign it 'Mohammed Al—' then suddenly, realising the error of his ways, he scored it out with the pen and began to write above it 'Abdul Ahmed'!

His lapse in concentration in forgetting who he was that day cost him dearly, but I bet he won't forget who he is next time he gets stopped by the police!

Who's Comforting Who?

. . .

George had arrived at my office from the Drug Squad, where he had worked for several years and, as you can imagine, had seen some memorable sights during his time there.

We both had the same years in service and on one particular day, we were detailed to work together.

During the shift, we received a 'death message' to deliver.

This was the sudden death of an older man, who had collapsed in the street going to the local post office.

His elderly wife, who had remained in the family home, was totally unaware and had to be informed.

As usual, in these difficult circumstances, you call at a relative, a neighbour or a friend's house, to ask them to accompany you to the family home and assist in comforting the person whom you are about to inform with the sad news regarding the death of a loved one.

Unable to trace a relative, we called at her neighbour's house and explained the situation.

The neighbour, who was also a close friend of the elderly couple, was devastated at the news but was prepared to accompany us.

We knocked on the door and the wife answered it.

'Hello, Mrs Brown, I wonder if we could come in a minute? We have some sad news to tell you,' I said to her.

'If it's about Paw Broon, he's at the shops getting a few messages, but he'll be back shortly!' she said in all innocence.

'Well, it is about "Paw", hen, but I'm afraid it's not very good news!'

By this time we had walked through to the living room area.

With the assistance of her neighbour to comfort her and

put an arm around her, I broke the news of her husband's sudden death.

There is no easy way to perform this task!

No book has ever been written describing how to go about it and it doesn't matter who you are – a family death is devastating!

The poor woman was distraught, the tears and cries of disbelief greeted us, as the neighbour, with tears in her eyes, tried along with George to console her.

I decided to make a cup of tea, while the others were comforting her.

As I was doing this, I noticed there was no milk.

I told the neighbour, who permitted me to go into her house and get some from the fridge in the kitchen.

What a shock there was for me when I returned to the grieving woman's house!

There in the middle of the sofa couch, was my police partner George, sobbing uncontrollably and being comforted by both the bereaved woman and her neighbour.

Looking at the situation, you'd have thought George was the one who had just received the bad news.

The older woman had her arm around George, patting him sympathetically and saying, 'It's OK, son, just let it all out and don't be embarrassed!'

I couldn't believe what I was seeing! I was lost for words!

So I blurted out the first thing that came into my head: 'That'll be three cups of tea, then? Milk and sugar, everybody?'

Later, once George had drunk his tea and composed himself, he told me that in his twenty-three years' police service, this was the first time he had ever delivered a death message to a loved one and the built-up emotion of it all had just hit him!

'Promise me you won't say anything to anyone about what occurred today!' he pleaded with me.

'My lips are sealed, George!' I replied, as I drew my fingers across my lips, as if to close a zip fastener.

However, the nickname Greetin' Face stuck with him for the rest of his police service.

To this day George thinks I said something – but I can assure him I didn't! I wrote it down!!

Road Accident Excuses

· · ·

'I was sure the old fellow would never make it to the other side of the road, so I struck him with my car.'

In the Dark

· · ·

During a recent football match at which I was engaged on duty in the stadium, I was standing on the touchline, near to the players' tunnel, when the floodlighting system went out, placing the entire stadium in total darkness.

The referee immediately summoned all the players on both sides to the centre circle and began to lead them off the park.

As the players filtered off towards the dressing room, the referee and his assistants were just about to enter the tunnel when a spectator in the crowd shouted, 'This shouldn't make any difference to you, referee – you've been in the dark all bloody night!!'

The Bar-L Strike

...

During a strike by prison officers at HMP Barlinnie in Glasgow, they were refusing to accept any more prisoners during the dispute.

As a result, the prisoners were being housed at police stations such as London Road.

Many police officers from the divisions around Glasgow were detailed to report there for their duties, these being to perform the job of prison warden.

Let me inform you immediately – both jobs are completely opposite and entail a different approach.

We had to allow the prisoners certain privileges not permitted in the 'Bar-L', in order to prevent any unwanted disturbances or rioting!

Whilst on this duty, I spoke with some of the prisoners and have enclosed a few of the conversations.

Alec: 'I'm fifty-eight years of age and I'm a lifer in instalments. I've served twenty-six years in prison for drink-related offences like breach of the peace, drunk and incapable and shoplifting, all stupid things because of my alcohol problem. I'm safe in here, because I can't handle the outside – I'm frightened!'

Alec died shortly after his release; his death was alcohol-related.

Ian: 'It's my first time in prison and I got locked up for litter! I threw a lousy chip poke away.'

'You don't get locked up for litter,' I said.

'You do if you fail to pay the fine!' he replied.

Tam: 'My brief said, "It's only breach of the peace, just plead guilty. Everybody's getting a letter to return to court after the prison dispute is resolved. You won't be sentenced today!"

'So what happened? With his expert advice, I pled guilty and was sentenced to thirty days!'

Later the same evening, Tam shouted out, 'Hey, boss, any chance of a wee stretch?'

I shouted back, 'You've already got thirty days, Tam, is that not enough for you?'

Is that a Cannon I Hear?

. . .

A young struggling actor was contacted by his agent and offered a part in the London West End play *Waterloo*.

The part was small, but the pay was very good and it would guarantee him some much-needed work for several months.

On accepting the offer, he was sent his lines to learn and told to come immediately to London. With his bags packed, he was off.

As he travelled down on the train, he tried out various voices to deliver his line: 'Hark! Is that a cannon I hear?'

This rehearsal continued all the way to the stage door of the theatre, as he arrived minutes prior to the start of the play and his big entrance.

He was quickly whisked off to make-up and wardrobe, dressed in costume and ready to walk on stage, with minutes to spare.

As he received his cue to make his entrance and say his line, he took several steps toward centre stage, when suddenly there was an almighty 'BANG!!'

Receiving such a fright, he totally forgot his opening line and blurted out loudly, 'WHAT THE FUCK WAS THAT?'

Trailer Bike

. . .

One day while out on motorcycle patrol, I passed a garden centre advertising a closing-down sale!

During my lunch break, I went in and it was Christmas for me.

Everything you'll ever want at ridiculously reduced prices – I just had to have some of this.

'I'll take six bags of that and four bags of this and four of your rowan trees. Oh! And give me four of your wild-bird houses and three packets of birdseed. Is that grass seed and lawn feed? I'll take some of them and two tins of fencing preservative paint and a hard garden brush and bucket!'

They even had that new Whyte and Mackay grass seed. You just scatter it over your lawn and it comes up half-cut!!

Anyway, after the assistant had totalled up the cost and I had paid for it all, I asked him, 'What time do you close and I'll come back and collect my goods later?'

'Sorry, mate!' he replied. 'We're closing now. You'll have to take it all with you!'

Arrghh! Shock horror!

Out I went to my police motorcycle and loaded the six bags of compost across the back pannier boxes, grass seed and lawn food in the pannier, bird food and boxes in the other pannier, paint tins balanced on top of both panniers, held by the weight of the compost bags, potting compost across the petrol tank, and I carried the trees and brush in one hand!

Down the road I went on my bike, camouflaged like a landscaped garden with my bargains.

Just as I was turning into the motorcycle shed, I was

passed by my superintendent in his car, who almost crashed as he spun his neck around like Linda Blair from *The Exorcist* for a look!

Later, I was reprimanded for my improper behaviour.

Next day I received a memo from him, instructing me to attend the motorcycle garage to have a trailer fitted to my bike, just in case I came across another closing-down sale.

Don't Talk to Strangers
...

One day I was sitting in the lounge of my house, having a glass of wine with my new next-door neighbour.

Suddenly the front door opened and in walked my youngest daughter, carrying an armchair.

A few minutes later, the door opened again and she was followed in by my other two kids, who were carrying a three-seater sofa between them.

I enquired where the items had come from.

To which my eldest daughter replied, 'A man gave them to us!'

I immediately got up from my seat and proceeded to scold all three of my kids.

'What are you doing?' asked my shocked and surprised new neighbour.

To which I replied, 'I'm fed up telling them, never take a suite off a stranger!!!'

Remind Me of Reminsky!

. . .

On hearing the news that a film is to be made about the life of the famous safebreaker Johnny Reminsky, I was reminded of a story I was told by a detective inspector.

As a young police probationer, he was patrolling his beat one night and checking out property in the area.

He went around the rear of a post office in Paisley Road, Glasgow, when he heard something.

He shone his torch up in the direction of the noise and saw a man sliding down a drainpipe at the rear of the building.

As he drew his police baton, the man said, 'Calm down, son. You've caught me fair and square. I won't give you any trouble!'

On reaching the ground level, he immediately held his hands out in front to be handcuffed by the young cop.

What a surprise to learn later that he had apprehended the famous gentleman safebreaker and war hero Johnny Reminsky!

Apparently Johnny was serving a prison sentence during the war and was released by the authorities to help the war effort.

He was flown to Germany, behind enemy lines, with specific orders to break into certain safes and steal enemy secrets!

By all accounts Johnny performed his duty to his usual perfection and proved no safe was safe from Johnny Reminsky!!

Marmalade or Jam?

...

I was fortunate to visit Moscow several times and struck up a relationship with a local Muscovite called Vitaly Mironov, who was a historian and president of the Moscow Caledonian Society.

One evening, whilst participating in a little drinky-poo of the local vodka, Vitaly told me a story about one of the first times he visited the United States.

He had frequented a bar-diner near to the hotel where he was staying and became the centre of attention with the regulars.

The conversation got around to sex and one of the American hippy-style guys, who had joined the company, asked Vitaly what methods they used when making love in Russia.

Vitaly, trying to sound interesting and knowledgeable to his new American friends, said in his best broken English: 'I always use preservative, I enjoy sex better!'

'Preservative?' asked the hippy, surprised by this.

'Yes, preservatives. And in Russia we have many types and fancy flavours!' he said, rather pleased with himself.

Several more drinks later, he made his excuses and headed back to his hotel for the night.

The following evening, he went back to the local bar-diner for a drink, and, as he walked in, the joint-smoking hippy guy who had been part of his company the previous evening shouted out:

'Hey, Boris, I tried your Russian way of having sex last night. It was amazing, man, my woman went wild! She loved the strawberry jelly preserve the best!'

However, now with a better knowledge and command

of the English language, he informed me he meant 'preventative' sex, as in a condom, as opposed to 'preservative', as in jam!

Wood U Beleeve It?

. . .

Whilst checking our missing person reports at the office, I was looking up a recent report involving a young girl, when I noticed an update from a young officer that stated: 'Her mother is unable to give any further information as she is dyslexic and cannot read or right.'

Neither could the writter updating this resort!

Road Accident Excuses

. . .

'I pulled away from the side of the road, glanced over at my mother-in-law and headed over the embankment.'

More New Releases

. . .

Strathclyde Police Pipe Band performed in a recent competition.

I'm informed they played a haunting melody.

'Haunting' because they were murdering it!

(Now they're just jokes, guys. You're not bad!)

Mini a Bargain

. . .

Being recognised as a bit of a scatter-cash, there was no expense spared when I purchased my first real motor car.

There it was, in the paper, circled with a fancy box, with the bold heading stating: 'Bargain of the Month!'

I liked the name right away, a Morris Mini, brown in colour and all for the princely sum of £30 cash, payable to the Executive Cars Centre, Paisley.

The pungent smell of dampness should have been an obvious clue, but I accepted the salesman's patter.

'Can ye no' smell that leather upholstery? Man, ye just cannae beat the real McCoy!' he enthused. 'And another extra feature fitted is the sporty bucket seats,' he added.

They were certainly bucket seats all right! Saturated with water and the metal handle still attached!

There was a 'Hole in dem buckets, dear Henry, dear Henry' . . .

The radio wasn't working, but he put it down to a faulty valve or maybe a short wire!

In other words, I think there was a wire–less!

'Don't worry, sir, we'll replace it!' he said with an air of confidence. 'Are we paying by cash or would you like credit arrangements?' he then enquired.

'None of your HP credit payments for me,' I said as I handed over my hard cash, £6 of which was made up with crisp new 10-shilling notes from my pay packet.

With the ignition key in my hand, I jumped into the driver seat and started it up.

In an instant, I noticed there was no 'va va voom!'

It was more like a 'buzz buzz buzzz!' For a brief moment I thought there was a wasp stuck up the exhaust pipe, but no, that was the noise from my 'souped-up' (clapped-out) engine.

'Just listen to that engine, man, it's purring like a cat,' said the drooling salesman, with his syrup or fig hairpiece slightly askew.

'Purring like a cat' my arse! It was more like 'squealing like a pork-belly pig'!

The noise emanating from under the bonnet suggested a slack fan belt. Or in my case, probably a slack snake belt!

Even the valid MOT certificate was a duplicate. The examiner obviously didn't believe it the first time!

However, I put all that to one side as I drove out on to the main road.

Let's see what this baby can do, I thought. Nought to sixty in eight, the salesman had said: he forgot to mention days, not seconds.

I should have remembered that old saying of my father's: 'The only good thing about Paisley, son, is the main road leading out of it to Glasgow!'

Well I was on it and I was eager to burn some rubber.

Forget Michael Schumacher – he was just a 'Cobbler' from the Govan area when I was at school!

With the pedal to the metal, I was off in a large puff of smoke. So much so, I actually expected a genie to appear and grant me three wishes. Like, 'I wish I had an engine', 'I wish I was a mechanic' and, thirdly, 'I wish I had a brain'!

Well it was the pantomime season after all. (Oh, yes it was!)

Having been on the road now for just over thirty minutes, enough time to go there and back on a bus and driving full out, I saw a sign for Glasgow.

The art of prayer really works.

Now, I know a Mini engine is not the most powerful, but this one of mine couldn't pull a sailor off yer granny! Suffice to say I would have been hard pushed to pull the skin off my Ambrosia creamed rice!

A man and woman on bicycles and an old woman pulling herself along in a wheelchair overtook me twice!

With one leg and a punctured tyre!

Come to think of it, maybe the holes in the floor of my car were for your Doc Marten feet to go through, so you could run and make it go faster. Then again, maybe they were for the braking system.

Suddenly, it began to rain quite heavily and I switched on the windscreen wipers . . . Nothing! Zilch! Nada! Zero!

They didn't work and as the rain got heavier, it became more difficult to see the road ahead.

Drastic times require drastic measures, as I rolled down my driver's window, put my hand out and, grabbing hold of the wipers, I began operating them manually, thrashing them up and down the windscreen. Not recommended!

To cut a very long story short, I decided not to hold on to it for too long.

Depreciation in value and all that.

So, while I was a student at the Police College, Tulliallan, I was offered the chance to purchase another Mini, this time from a sergeant, Colin Robertson, who was a college instructor.

As they say in Glasgow, it was 'minted'! So, after checking the windscreen wipers worked properly, I bought it!

Here I was, twenty-one years of age, the Jeremy Clarkson of Govan and the first two-car family in the street. Mind you, there were only two houses: it was an awfy wee street I lived in.

Was I becoming an obsessed collector of cars, I thought?

As it was, Dougie Mack, a fellow student, was also looking for some form of transport and practically begged me to sell my manually operated Mini.

Without too much persuasion, I managed to convince him to talk me into selling him my wee passion wagon.

'OK! OK!' I said, reluctantly. 'Give me thirty quid cash and she's yours.'

Why call it 'she'? 'Cause it was an absolute cow in the morning! Plus the rest of the entire day, I might add.

I had to tinker about with the engine just to start it.

It was like performing foreplay, before I could get it to do anything.

However, Dougie was a single guy and had money burning a hole in his pocket.

I couldn't help but smile when, driving down the motorway on my way home from Tulliallan for the weekend, I was overtaken by Dougie, waving away frantically and blasting the horn with excitement as he passed.

I think that was the first time it had passed anything.

I tell a lie, it passed water the day the radiator hose burst, but therein lies another story!

On returning to the police college the following Monday, I had to laugh when I asked Dougie how the car was running and he informed me it had been scrapped!

'Scrapped?' I said, somewhat hesitant and surprised.

'Aye, I gave a burd a lift home from the dancing on Friday night and as I was reversing, listening to Suzi Quatro on the radio, I bumped into an Audi Quatro!'

'Whit! Her man?' I enquired.

'No! Another motor in the car park. Bashed in the driver's door. That cost me an arm and a leg,' he said.

'What about your damage?' I asked.

'My damage?' he replied. 'The bloody sub-frame collapsed, but the burd was a darling, so I ignored it and drove along a country road and parked up in a field for a wee winching session, while we listened to Wet Wet Wet.

'As it turned out, it was more like "Pish Pish Pish" as the rain became heavier and poured down.

'Later, as I went to drive away, the ground was that soft with all the rain, the bloody Mini had sunk and was up to the axles in mud.

'So I'm stuck fast in the mud and had to call out a recovery vehicle company, who proceeded to rip me off along with the rest of the sub-frame, as he towed my Mini out of the field.

'Total cost for my weekend: thirty quid to you for the motor, a hundred quid to the Audi driver for the damage to his door and forty quid for the recovery driver, and as if that wasn't enough, I never even got my Nat King Cole!!'

As he stood staring at me, I said sympathetically, 'Ah well, Dougie, some people are just lucky with cars. Some people are just lucky in love. But unfortunately for you, Dougie . . .'

I paused for a moment, then said, 'You've just got too much money!'

What's Perjury?

• • •

During a trial in the Glasgow Sheriff Court, a witness was called to give evidence for the defence.

The accused in the dock just happened to be a very good friend of the witness and, when questioned by the procurator fiscal, he became very evasive and flippant in his answers.

The procurator fiscal, who was by this time becoming annoyed and fed up with the witness and his lack of genuine response to his questions, said to him, 'Let me remind you that you took an oath to tell the truth, the whole truth and nothing but the truth!'

The witness replied indignantly, 'I am well aware of that, sir!'

'Well,' said the procurator fiscal, 'and are you well aware of what you can get for perjury?'

As quick as a flash, the witness replied, 'Aye, about twenty thousand a year, if you're a polis!'

Control Room Story

• • •

When I was a motorcycle cop, I received the following call from the control room: 'AS Control calls Tango Charlie One Four to attend and assist in the removal of a stolen Suzuki motorcycle, recovered abandoned in Queen Street, Glasgow. Please note, there is a policewoman standing by it.'

I then enquired from the controller, 'Tango Charlie One Four, is it rideable?'

To which the controller replied, 'Affirmative, Tango Charlie One Four, and she's not bad-looking either!!'

Road Accident Excuses

. . .

'Coming home, I drove into the wrong house and collided with a tree I don't have in my driveway.'

Hello, Dolly

. . .

One day while I was engaged in uniform police duties in the office, I had occasion to answer the telephone to a chief inspector from the Discipline Department, requesting to speak with another officer in the station.

The officer concerned was always playing practical jokes on the younger members in the office and would boast about what he had done to them.

With this in mind and eager to turn the tables on him for showing off, I pressed the mute button on the desk telephone and summoned the boaster concerned, aptly named Gattling Gub.

I informed him that his wife was on the telephone wishing to speak with him!

I then released the mute button as he snatched the telephone from my hand and promptly blurted out, 'Hello, doll, what can I do for you?'

To which the chief inspector replied, 'Well, you can refer to me as sir for a start!!'

As for me, I got great satisfaction from his body language as I watched him with telephone in one hand, squirming to attention!

Road Accident Excuses

· · ·

'In an attempt to kill a fly, I drove into a telephone pole.'

Lost for Words

· · ·

One day out on the main street of the area I worked, a bus driver friend of my brother's approached me.

I remarked about how tanned he was and he said he was just back from a family holiday.

He then added that while away on holiday, he had lost his father.

Not immediately realising what he meant, I said, 'Don't tell me – a pub crawl. I'm the same, it's that cheap foreign plonk, it gives me the "Tex Ritters"—'

At this point he interrupted me and said, 'No, Harry, when I say I lost him, I mean, he died!'

Oops!!

Road Accident Excuses

· · ·

'A truck reversed through my windscreen into my wife's face.'

DNA Not Required

...

A senior cop receives a call to attend a suspicious death in an ice-cream café.

Accompanied by a young raw recruit, he makes his way to the location.

On arrival, they walk into the café and are shown by the proprietor to the location of the body.

The senior cop turns to the young recruit and says, 'Right, have a look and tell me what you see.'

The young cop bends down, looks at the body and says, 'His legs, from his feet to his hips, are covered in ice cream!'

'OK,' says the senior cop. 'Have another good look.'

The young cop bends down again to look.

'From his waist to his shoulders, he's covered in a sticky raspberry sauce!'

'Good,' says the senior cop. 'Now have one more thorough look and tell me if you know the cause of death.'

He bends down for a third time, studies the body, then stands up and says, 'His head is covered with flaked chocolate!'

'So what does that tell you about how he died, then?' asked the senior cop.

'Simple,' replied the young officer. 'He topped himself!!'

Crime Doesn't Always Pay

...

A would-be thief entered a well-established clothing store and after perusing the clothing rails for several minutes, he picked out a pair of trousers that appeared to take his fancy.

Dressed in an old pair of denim jeans, he asked the assistant to direct him to the changing room to try them on.

As the store was relatively busy, the assistant couldn't remain with him and left to tend to another customer.

However, when the assistant returned a short time later, the male had eloped with the trousers, leaving behind his old denim jeans.

Having been duped by the thief, the manager was about to mark it down to another theft for statistics, when he noticed a slight bulge in the back pocket of the jeans.

It turned out to be a leather wallet which contained £65 in cash.

The loss became a profit, as the trousers had a price tag of only £24.99.

This was one thief who learned the hard way that crime doesn't pay and, at this rate, it wouldn't be long before he became bankrupt!!

Who Was That?

. . .

Whilst working in the police motor vehicle garage at the start of my traffic patrol officer career, I was being shown all the various parts of a car engine, what can go wrong and how to repair it. Like I was remotely interested!

Later the same day, I was walking down to the end of the garage, when the wall telephone started ringing.

The garage sergeant shouted for me to answer it, so I went over and picked it up and the following is what took place.

'Helen Street police Garage, can I help you?'

'Yes, you can,' replied the caller. 'You can tell me what is happening with the nightshift superintendent's car.'

'I have absolutely no idea what's happening with it!' I replied.

To which the caller responded, 'Do you know who you are speaking too?'

'No,' I replied. 'Who am I speaking too?'

'You are speaking with Superintendent McKinlay!' he said.

'And do you know who *you're* speaking to?' I said rather indignantly.

'No, I don't,' he answered.

To which I replied, 'Good!' and promptly put the telephone down.

'Who was that, Harry?' enquired the garage sergeant.

'Just a wrong number!' I said as I quickly walked off.

The Adventures of Harry the Polis

Smoking Cough

· · ·

During a social night out at the police club, I was sitting at a table opposite another couple.

Later the same evening, the woman began to cough and splutter.

This went on for several minutes, with the coughing becoming more intense, as the woman's face changed colour and as I looked over at her, she appeared to be choking and unable to draw a breath.

I quickly left my seat and ran over to assist her. 'Watch! I'm trained in first aid,' I said.

Grabbing hold of her head, I promptly pushed it down between her legs and held it there.

Suddenly she stopped coughing and began screaming and howling hysterically, waving her arms in serious distress.

Well! How was I to know she had a lit cigarette in her mouth?

Barber's

· · ·

A police officer walked into a barber's and asked for a haircut and a shave.

The barber cut his hair and then began to shave him. As he did so, he nicked him with the razor.

'Your face is familiar, have I shaved you before?' the barber asked.

'Yes,' replied the cop. 'But it's healed up since then!'

The Job's Fucked

• • •

A regular saying in the police force was, 'The job's fucked,' from the many disgruntled Glasgow police officers during the early seventies.

Every other week, a police officer, using the all-systems radio airways, would interrupt the occasional silence, by broadcasting to all mobile and radio stations, 'The job's fucked!'

One particular day, an assistant chief constable was in the HQ radio control room when over the radio came the aforesaid, 'The job's fucked!'

The assistant chief constable, on hearing this announcement, immediately picked up the radio handset and broadcast,

'Would the station whom has just transmitted that statement, please identify yourself?'

The same voice replied, 'What for? The job's fucked!'

Getting frustrated by this anonymous caller and his remark on air, the assistant chief constable again broadcast, but this time he identified himself:

'This is Assistant Chief Constable Bennie. Would the officer transmitting that last statement please identify yourself to me?'

To which the caller paused for a moment before replying in a droll voice, 'It's no' that fucked!!'

Now That's Magic

• • •

One evening, along with my partner Ewan Cameron, I was on mobile patrol when I stopped a car for having a rear tail light out.

I informed the driver why I had stopped him and he got out of his car and went to the rear to check for himself.

While doing this, Cameron walked to the front of the car to check for any other obvious defects.

The driver, meanwhile, on seeing the defective rear light, lifted his foot and kicked the light cover a few times, at which point, due to faulty wiring, the light came back on.

He then looked at me with a smug grin on his face and said, 'There ye go, as if by magic! It just needed a wee kick in the right place!'

At which point Cameron said, 'Good for you, mate. Now would you like to try that trick on your windscreen and see if you can get a tax disc to appear?'

Now, that *would* be magic!!

Canteen

• • •

Big Eddie Oliver walks into the police canteen and is approached by the counter assistant, Cathy, who says, 'I have braised kidneys, boiled tongue, fried liver and pig's feet!'

Big Eddie replies, 'Don't tell me your medical health problems, Cathy, just give me something to eat!'

Bad Breath

• • •

The morning after a heavy night out, where everybody had gorged themselves with food and drunk the pub dry, a CID officer called into the station for a cup of coffee and a quick cure for a severe hangover.

As he approached me, he said, 'Harry, can I have a cup of your coffee to make me feel better?'

To which I replied, 'On one condition, Bob! You could go outside and eat a dog's turd and tone your breath down a bit!! Now that would make me feel better!!'

No Profit in Theft

• • •

A man walked into a shop and placed a £20 note on the counter.

He then asked the assistant for change of the note.

The cashier duly obliged and opened the cash drawer.

Quick as a flash, the man put his hand into the till and grabbed what money he could before running off out of the shop into the street, leaving behind the £20 note he had placed on the counter.

On checking the contents of the shop cash register, it was discovered the thief had snatched the total sum of . . . £14.

Thereby making the thief a loss of £6 and the shopkeeper a profit of £6.

This is one robber who would be well advised to start going straight and work for a living!

Who's a Boot?

. . .

I was contacted one day to return to the station and perform an urgent escort duty.

On my arrival back at the station, the sergeant instructed me to take a CID car and drive over to police headquarters and collect a policewoman called Delia Blain, to accompany me with the transport of a female prisoner.

I arrived at police HQ and walked into the front office, where I enquired from the police control room staff, in my broadest Glaswegian accent, 'Is Delia aboot?'

To which one of the cops replied, 'No, she is not. In fact, she's quite a nice girl!!'

Single White Male

. . .

A young ginger-haired, spotty-faced police recruit called in at his local Asda store.

As he got to the checkout, he placed a loaf of bread, a pint of milk and a can of beans on the conveyor belt.

The pretty cashier looked up at him as she scanned his goods.

'Are you single?' she asked him.

'Yeah!' he replied. 'How did you know?'

To which the pretty cashier said, ''Cause you're an ugly bastard!'

Toilet Paper

· · ·

It's amazing how they now talk about recycling refuse.

Way back in the fifties and sixties everybody in the street where I lived did it. In those days it was called 'nae lavvy paper'!

None of your Velvet, Andrex, 'soft tissue', 'quilted' or any other crap for us, pardon the pun! That wee Labrador dog wasn't even born then.

Now, if you were posh and could afford it, you used Izal!

Its slippery surface didn't wipe your arse, it just spread it further than Flora margarine.

No wonder they wrote, 'Now wash hands please'! Yer hands? Ye had to have a bath after it!

As for my family, it was the *Daily Record* cut into neat squares! However, it was the *Evening Citizen* for any visitors! Pure class!

Ladies and Gents, No Bother

· · ·

Several years ago, the shift I was working on organised a day out with all of our kids at a local swimming club.

I shared a locker with my young son, and my two daughters, aged ten and five, did likewise.

Later, after we had left the pool and had a shower, my two daughters were drying themselves when the youngest one, Kimmy, decided to go to the toilet.

Out she went from the shared cubicle, only to return several minutes later to ask her older sister, 'Samantha, am I a male or a female?'

Straight from the Horse

...

During a drugs trial in Glasgow, a senior detective was cited as an expert witness to clarify that the amount of drugs found on an accused person was being used to supply drug deals and not, as the defence claimed, for his personal use.

The defence agent continued to press the point that the drugs were for his client's own personal use.

The senior detective however, in his role as an expert witness for the Crown, was reiterating his response that when cut into equal quantities, it was a clear indication it was for supplying drug deals.

The detective continued that if it were for personal use, there would be no need to cut or divide it into equal parts.

However, the defence agent persisted with his client's futile excuse about personal use and pursued this line of questioning.

Finally the sheriff, bored by this continual line of questioning, interrupted the defence agent and in a stern voice asked, 'Excuse me, Mr Carr, but, have you ever been charged with cruelty to animals?'

The defence agent looked up at the sheriff on the bench and with a puzzled expression enquired, 'Why, m'lord?'

To which the sheriff responded, 'Because you're flogging a dead horse. Now let's move on!!'

Kiss Me Quick

• • •

In 1976, at the Police International Tattoo in the Kelvin Hall Arena in Glasgow, I was performing a routine display with the rest of the motorcycle section.

However, prior to our performance, we had to take turns on the police motorcycle stand and answer questions from members of the public, as well as giving children a seat on the police motorbike or in a traffic patrol car.

When I was on the stand taking my turn, a young female civilian staff member of the Traffic Police Administration Department entered the stand and tapped me on the shoulder.

On seeing her, I put my arms around her and took her in a passionate embrace, leaned her over the motorcycle saddle and proceeded to give her a long, deep, sensual kiss. (As a joke.)

As we straightened up again, I noticed she had a stunned expression on her face and was blushing uncontrollably.

For a moment, I thought I had swooned her off her feet, but to my total embarrassment and humiliation she said, 'Harry, I'd like you to meet my dad and my brother!'

I turned around to see two men, six feet tall, glaring at me!

The Battery Store

. . .

Out one day on patrol, my partner Kenny was telling me his car battery was flat and he wanted to go along to the police garage in Helen Street to charge it up.

When we arrived, Kenny went to see Alex, the garage sergeant, and asked his permission to charge his car battery.

Alex said, 'Yeah, on you go, but d'you know how to do it?'

Kenny replied confidently, 'No problem, I've seen the set-up!'

Off he went, carrying his car battery along to the battery store.

On entering the store, there must have been about thirty to forty large car batteries, all connected up to each other and all being charged at the same time.

While I looked around at the complicated system linking all the batteries together, Kenny lifted his battery up into a space on the shelf.

He then took the positive and negative wire leads and connected the negative lead to the battery beside his and then took the positive and clipped it on to his battery . . .

Bang! The battery next to his exploded and within seconds, there was a chain reaction – Bang! Bang! Bang! Bang!

The entire battery store resembled the fourth of July!

Three and four at a time, every battery in the store was exploding round about us, as we were showered in acid and bits off the exploding batteries!

I quickly did a runner, leaving big Kenny with a helluva job to do in explaining his obviously serious mistake to Alex!

I'll Tell Him Tomorrow, Maybe!

...

One evening, a well-dressed male accountant picked up a young prostitute from the red-light district of Blythswood Square in Glasgow.

Having agreed a price for full sex, he drove off with her in his car to her home on the Southside of the city.

They both stripped off and engaged in sexual intercourse, after which, while she was in the toilet washing, the accountant got dressed and quickly left the house, neglecting to pay the prostitute the agreed fee for the services she had provided.

Not to be outdone so easily, the aggrieved female contacted her minder, who just happened to be in the vicinity.

Armed with a baseball bat, he confronted the accountant as he made his way out of the high-rise tower block, en route to his parked car.

The accountant displayed some wonderful athletic skills and ran like hell, pursued by 'Babe Ruth', armed with the baseball bat.

At this point an anonymous call was made to the police station regarding one male being pursued by another, armed with a large club.

A police car was immediately dispatched to attend the call, whereby, on their arrival, they quickly observed and apprehended Babe Ruth.

Handcuffing him, they placed him in the rear of the police car, while they obtained a full statement about the incident from the shaken accountant.

Whilst noting the statement, one of the officers was beckoned over by a woman in the large assembled crowd.

It was the young prostitute who had been involved.

She then related to the officer her side of the story with regards to the events that had taken place earlier.

Armed with this new information, the officer returned to the accountant, who immediately blurted out, 'Whatever she said, she's lying, she's a lying little whore!'

The officer then related her story, as told to him.

The smug accountant then freely admitted giving her a lift home because she had looked unwell, but strenuously denied being involved with her in any sexual act. In fact, he went as far as to say, 'I did not have sexual relations with that woman.'

(Where have I heard that line before, Bill?)

'She's a lying little whore, but then, what do you expect from the residents about this area?' he replied rather indignantly.

The officer then said, facetiously, 'You're right enough, sir, who ever heard of an accountant cheating a client out of their money?' He paused for a moment before continuing, 'Anyway, sir, I have to ask you a question! You definitely deny having had sexual intercourse with her?'

'I certainly do! What do you take me for? I'm a happily married man!' the accountant responded with his pitiful denial.

'Well, sir!' replied the officer. 'I'm ever so glad to hear you say that, because apparently she's been diagnosed HIV positive and she continues to entertain men in her flat for unprotected sexual intercourse!'

On hearing this, the accountant's facial expression changed, as the colour visibly drained from his face.

'Are you OK, sir?' asked the officer. 'You look like a ghost!'

The accountant replied very quietly, 'Not really. I'm feeling a bit nauseous and would just like to go home to my wife and my family now!'

'But what about Babe Ruth with the baseball bat? We haven't charged him yet,' said the officer.

The accountant replied, 'I'm not interested. I'd like to drop all the charges against him and go home please. I'm feeling very ill with all this!'

'I'm not surprised, sir, but are you sure, because he looks really nasty with that big baseball bat?' said the condescending officer.

'Yes, I'm positive, now can I just go home please? I've wasted enough time here,' the accountant said.

'Not a problem, sir. Just sign my notebook to the effect that you don't want to proceed with the charges,' said the officer. 'No harm done, so by all means, you can go on your way now!'

The accountant then walked off rather unsteadily to his car before getting in and driving off.

The first officer then said to the second officer, 'You might have told him you were only kidding about the HIV stuff!'

To which the first officer replied, 'What for? You heard him give the Bill Clinton speech – "I did not have sexual relations with that woman!" Now why would I disbelieve the lying, cheating bastard!'

PS: If you're the accountant involved and reading this, remove that rope from around your neck. It was only a joke!

Road Accident Excuses

• • •

'I was on my way to the doctor with rear end trouble when my universal joint gave way, causing me to have an unplanned accident.'

A Secret Service

• • •

This is a story I just had to include.

It has nothing to do with the police, but refers to my son Scott, who was six years old at the time and was fascinated with his hero James Bond.

One Sunday afternoon, having attended church in the morning, we were relaxing at home when the telephone rang.

Quick as a flash, my son Scott answered, 'Hello, James Bond here!'

The person at the other end of the line paused for a moment, then said, 'Is that you, Scott?'

Slightly puzzled by the caller, Scott answered, 'Yes!'

'Do you know who this is?' enquired the caller.

Still puzzled, Scott replied, 'No!'

The caller responded by saying, 'Well, I spoke to you this morning in church! Now do you know who it is?'

Scott paused for a moment, then replied, 'Is it you, God?'

He was nearly right. It was the minister!

Wanted

...

Several years ago my oldest daughter Samantha, who would be about five or six at the time, was out playing in the front garden when a car drove past at speed and the driver stuck his tongue out at her.

This really upset her and she ran into the house to tell me. I listened to her intently and then said I would look out for him when I was out on police patrol and deal with him severely.

My daughter was delighted with this response from her policeman dad.

Next day, she returned from school. 'That's him, Dad!' she said, handing me this sketch of the suspect responsible for sticking his tongue out at her, for me to hand out to my colleagues:

WANTED

As you can see from her excellent artist's sketch, he is instantly recognisable and extremely da-da-da-damn ugly!

Yuill and Dodds

• • •

This poem was written during the mineworkers' strike, April 1984.

Yuill and Dodds (Haulage) were contracted to play a big part and were escorted to and from Ravenscraig and Hunterston, when fully laden, in convoy by uniformed police car and motorcycle patrols.

Money for Old Coke

I love my Morris Minor though it's 25 years old.

I take it out on Sundays if the weather's not too cold.

We took it out on Sunday last, the wife, the weans and me

And drove along the Fenwick Moor for a picnic by the sea.

We admired the lovely countryside, truly the work of Gods,

When thundering around a corner came a fucking Yuill and Dodds!

As it trundled up towards us, its size just grew and grew.

I had visions of having 'Scania' stamped across my brew.

As the lorry thundered past me I thought my life had endit!

Wait till I get my hands on him, that trucking Mexican bandit.

The coal dust was just clearing from the bandit's little ploy

When coming straight towards me was the Ravenscraig convoy.

Now Yuill and Dodds are well-renowned from here to Timbuctoo –

The polis were always stopping them for things they shouldn't do.

But now the tables are turned and they're buddies every one,

A polis car goes out in front and leads them on their run.

Now the miners aren't very pleased the way they drive a truck –

None of them will ever stop 'cause they just don't give a fuck.

The drivers now are all caged in, I don't know how they stick it,

But I hear they're on a bonus if they hit-and-run a picket.

Yuill and Dodds will run for ever, I hear the people say,

And when the miners realise this, perhaps they'll call it a day.

So come on, boys, throw in the towel and let's just see it endit.

We've been counting up our money and now we'd like to spend it.

(Many police officers disagreed with the apparent taking of sides in this political dispute and also the views of miners' leader Arthur Scargill.)

Cobblers

• • •

A prisoner was released after serving twenty-five years in prison.

As he went through his property, he found a receipt in his jacket pocket for a cobbler's.

He went to the repair shop and handed it over to the cobbler, who studied it carefully.

'A pair of brown brogues, to be soled and heeled?' he asked.

'Yeah, that's correct!' said the prisoner.

'Be ready, Friday!' said the cobbler.

New Release

• • •

I have just been informed that the Strathclyde Police Pipe Band are to release a new CD of Scotland's finest bagpipe tunes.

The only hold-up is what to call it.

How about *Criminal*?

Speed Camera Excuse

• • •

'I was suffering from a heavy cold and sneezed excessively, causing a chain reaction whereby my foot pushed down harder on my accelerator, causing me to speed up at the wrong time.'

Everything is Free

. . .

One day in the office, we were in the process of organising a night out for the entire shift to attend.

We were all chipping in with various venues to contact and arrange our do!

One place was too expensive for drink, or the food another served wasn't very good, or there was a severe lack of burds.

Then out of the blue Andy Kouskous, the shift sergeant, piped up, 'We could go to that new place that has opened up in Hamilton!'

'Do you know if it's good grub and cheap booze?' asked Jim.

'What's the talent like?' enquired Big Alan.

'Well,' said Andy, 'apparently, you get supplied with free cigarettes all night. You get free drink bought for you all night and the food menu is available for you to eat what you want, when you want and that's also absolutely free as well!! But – this is the best bit – at the end of the night, you can get as much nookie as you want!'

The guys were all dumfounded with this news, then one of them, slightly puzzled by this offer, asked, 'Who exactly told you all this, Andy?'

To which Andy proudly replied, 'My sister!!!'

Three in a Bed

. . .

Fed up with the many men-only nights that their police husbands and boyfriends were having, the partners decided it was their turn to have a ladies' night.

One of the wives took charge of organising it and had a video selection leaflet from her local video shop. In it, she had noticed a video called *Three in a Bed*, and having discussed it with the other partners, they unanimously agreed this was the video for their blue ladies' night.

They all arranged to meet at the home of the wife responsible for organising the video.

They also agreed that everyone attending should supply their own particular choice of alcohol for the occasion.

The big night duly arrived and all the excited ladies had assembled at the designated house.

They eagerly passed the video around, with the title *Three in a Bed* boldly displayed for all to see.

Was it two women and one man or two men and one woman?

Their imaginations were running wild and they couldn't wait to find out!

All eyes were on the operator as she stooped over to insert the video cassette. There was a moment of sheer anticipation from the excited ladies.

As they focused on the screen, a huge sigh of disappointment filled the room, as up on the screen before their very eyes came the words: 'Starring former world champions Jocky Wilson, Eric Bristow and Phil "the Power" Taylor.'

They had picked up an exhibition darts video!!

None of your 69s here, but there were plenty of, 'One hundred and eighty!'

Religious Exams

. . .

During the Traffic advanced driving exam at Tulliallan Police College, my colleague Willie Smith was filling out the questionnaire attached to his exam paper with his name, divisional number, registered number, etc.

Just below this, it asked for you to write down your 'region' and Willie, having misread it, wrote down 'Protestant'! Much to the amusement of the instructors and his fellow students.

Make Me Go Faster

. . .

My partner David Ball and I went over to the Police Federation office so that David could buy a pair of police sunglasses, which they sold at a very competitive price.

In he went while I waited outside.

I could see him trying on several pairs until he was satisfied.

Out he came, smiling like a poor man's Tom Cruise and wearing his new 'make me drive faster' sunglasses.

As he was about to get into the police Land Rover, I asked him to adjust the wing mirror on his passenger side.

Placing the sunglasses on his seat, he duly jumped out and obliged, before jumping back into the Land Rover and forgetting where he had left the sunglasses. He planted his big fat arse on top of his brand new sunglasses, breaking them!!

Football Detail

· · ·

One evening the traffic department were all reporting for football detail, when a big football match was taking place in Glasgow. Before, during and after the match, we all had specific duties to perform.

Having been instructed of my duties, my partner Jimmy McNulty and I went out to our patrol area.

Whilst driving along a road, near to the stadium, with parked cars lining either side of the well-lit road, I saw a sports car coming towards us from the opposite direction.

Jimmy, who was driving the police car at the time, began to move more and more into the centre of the road, in order to restrict the space of the oncoming vehicle.

Due to this action, the opposing driver was forced to stop.

Jimmy then drove up to the driver's window and asked him if he was in a hurry.

The driver replied that he was, as he was on his way to work.

Jimmy then said, 'Well, you'll save some time when you get there. You won't need to switch off your car lights.'

Then, as Jimmy started to drive off, he remarked just loud enough for the driver to hear, 'You wanker!'

The driver, looking at his dashboard to see why his lights were not on, then suddenly realised what Jimmy had just called him.

At that point he leant out of his car window and shouted after us, 'I'll wank you!'

To which Jimmy shouted back, 'Not tonight, darling, I'm on the football detail!!!'

Licensed to Bleed

. . .

On another occasion with Jimmy, we stopped a car for failing to comply with a red light and driving through the junction.

We immediately pursued and stopped the male offender.

As was normal, Jimmy spoke with the driver, checking his details while I walked around the vehicle looking for any obvious defects.

As I got to the front of the car, I saw Jimmy punch the driver full in the face and, as the driver threw himself back on to the passenger seat, Jimmy then tried to go through his open window to get at him.

I quickly grabbed Jimmy around the waist and pulled him away, while he protested vigorously.

I managed to calm him down – as far as was possible – and got him to sit in the police car, where he explained what had happened.

It seems that, when Jimmy asked the driver to produce his wee red-book driving licence, the driver had turned away for a moment before producing a licence containing two £1 notes inside.

Jimmy enquired what the money was for and the driver, out of the range of my view and hearing, said, 'It's yours – take it!'

This attempt at bribery completely flipped Jimmy into action.

As it was, Jimmy sent the driver away looking like something from Comic Relief with a real bloody red nose for his bother!

Mind you, with Wee Jimmy, the red nose was donated completely free of charge!

Roast Chicken and Chips

. . .

I think all the resident nutcases in the areas where I worked waited until I was on nightshift so that they could pay me a visit at the police station for free counselling sessions, followed by a cigarette, a cup of tea and a chocolate biscuit.

At one point, I was performing so many counselling sessions I thought I was employed by the NHS.

One of my regular visitors was a larger-than-life woman called Georgina Hill, or Georgie, as she preferred to be called.

Georgie was a big woman in every sense of the word and she was not blessed with the best of looks. When she put her make-up on, she had a face like a Hallowe'en cake. Obviously a lack of mirrors in the house.

She was excessively overweight by several stone and, stuffed into a tweed coat that was too small for her, she resembled a burst sofa!

Now that I have dispensed with the pleasantries, I will relate my story to you.

The station door opened just after midnight and in walked Georgie, larger than life.

'Hello, Mr Morris. Just popped in to see how you are and have a wee blether with you!' she said.

'I'm fine, thanks, Georgie. What about yourself? I haven't seen you around for a few weeks,' I replied.

That was my first big mistake of the night! It was the cue for Georgie to relate to me her entire medical history, pausing only to catch a breath!

'Well, I don't think I told you but I've been in hospital! I was suffering from a bit of woman trouble!'

She then proceeded to do a Les Dawson and Roy Barraclough impersonation, followed by a mime-artist impression as she pointed to her fat belly!

'All oot! All oot!' she cried as she made hand signs across her stomach like she was a paid-up member of the Masonic Lodge.

Her voice became quieter and her actions more animated – her operation sounded all the more serious.

'Anyway!' she continued, 'the surgeon opened me up right across my stomach and done the business. I was that wide open they had to call in an upholsterer to staple my wound together. The nurses said, "Georgie, what a mess you were in, hen! That was major woman problems you had." D'you know, Harry, see efter that operation, I was bloody ravishing. I could've eaten a scabby cat 'atween two slice of stale bread—'

I interrupted her. 'I think you mean ravenous, Georgie!'

'Same thing, Harry!' she said dismissively. 'Anyway, the staff nurse said, "I'm sorry, Georgie, but ye cannae eat. You'll need to wait for the doctor to come round first." Then they started all the small talk with me, like, "Have you got any kids, Georgie?" and "Are they boys or lassies?"

'Well, bugger me! Pardon my expression, but by this time my stomach thinks that my throat's been cut during the operation and all they can talk aboot is kids! Now, don't get me wrong, Harry, I love kids and right at that moment I could probably have eaten a whole wan tae myself! But right then all I'm thinking about is Colonel Sanders' Kentucky Fried Chicken – I'd even have plucked the thing myself!

'Anyways, next thing is the nurse tells me they have a special surprise for me. "What is it?" I'm thinking to myself. Has the surgeon removed the wrong orgasms? Has he lost his Rolex watch? Or maybe they've found bits of Shergar, 'cause that butcher on the main street is definitely dodgy – or maybe he just fancies me. "Gonnae put me oot my bloody misery and tell me?" I said to them.

'They both looked at each other for a moment before the staff nurse said, "Right, after you've had a nice hot bath, I've arranged for the kitchen staff to make your favourite meal – roast chicken and chips, just for you!"

' "Oh, ya wee dancer!" I said. "I hope it's the size of an ostrich 'cause I'm feeling pure anorexic!" Well, you never seen anybody get in and oot a bath as quick as me and when I looked at my old Jean Brodie, with all they staples across it, I resembled a centre page of wan o' my wean's school jotters! It was the first time I had seen myself in a full-length mirror and my big jazz drum was sticking oot like a pigeon's landing board! I kid you not – you could've balanced a tray o' drinks on my erse! Anyway, I'm diverting again. However, I'm oot the bath and I'm drying myself and just as I lifted my left leg up tae dry my feet – guess whit?'

She then performed her Les Dawson impression again and started mouthing, 'Some o' the staples started popping and I thought I was gonnae burst oot all over the floor.' ('God forbid!' – that's me thinking to myself!)

'Ah shouted for the nurses, but it was really another upholsterer I needed. The nurses came rushing in and whisked me away – I had to get emergency treatment. Well, next thing I know they've put me on a drip and gave me an emergency blood transmission to replace what I had lost! As if that wasn't enough, the nurse then tells me, "I'm sorry, Georgie, but you can't have anything to eat!"

'I said, "Whit! Are you yanking my chain? I've had that "Nil by mouth" sign up on my bed that long, my family thinks that's my real name in French!"

'Just at that the auxiliary nurse comes over to me and asks, "Do you need a bed pan, Georgie?"

' "Are you trying to take the piss?" I said sarcastically. "You need to eat before you can excrete!" I then turned my attention back to the nurse and said, "And who is going to get my roast chicken and chips, then?"

' "The bin," she replied. "The cook threw it out!" Now, as she put her arm across to tidy my bed sheet I thought about biting it aff!'

Just at that point there was a noise as the rear door of the station was opened and I could hear my colleagues coming in for their tea break.

Interrupting Georgie in full flow, I said, 'Well, Georgie, I could sit and listen to you going through your medical history all night, but I'll need to interrupt you because that's the boys in the police panda arriving for their refreshment period and you'll never guess what I'm going to have for my dinner.'

She stared at me for a moment before a smile broke out across her face and she said in an excited voice, 'Roast chicken and chips!'

To which I replied, 'No, three quarters of an hour like everybody else! Good night, Georgie!'

Forensic Psychologist
· · ·

A case at the High Court in Glasgow involved a carer looking after clients with learning disabilities. It was alleged that the carer was taking some of his clients into a secured room where he showed them pornographic videos. It was also alleged that he had sexually abused some of them!

Unable to understand the procedures of the court, the witnesses/complainers had to be taken in separately, prior to the court sitting, to let them see the inside of the courtroom. The judge also made himself available to meet with them and ask them a few simple questions, to confirm that they knew the difference between what is the truth and what is a lie!

Once they had satisfied the various wigs in the court that they knew the difference, the case for the prosecution commenced.

During the evidence a major part of the case relied on the testimony of a forensic psychologist who had interviewed the witnesses and the defence forensic psychologist who had studied his report.

The defence forensic psychologist identified herself to the court, citing her list of rather impressive qualifications.

Her evidence was critical of the prosecution psychologist's report and the methods he had used in obtaining his results, the main objection being that the prosecution psychologist had, on occasion, to repeat some questions to the victims during the examination.

Out of twelve questions asked of each victim, at least eight required to be repeated.

Thereby, in the defence expert's opinion, repeating the

questions to the victims had prompted totally different answers.

She also stated that due to the method used, each of the alleged victims had been scaled higher in their mental ability and understanding than they should have been!

The advocate depute representing the prosecution then stood up and began the cross-examination of the defence's expert witness.

It was noticeable that each time she asked a question she turned and looked towards the jury at the opposite side of the courtroom, thereby not addressing her questions directly at the defence witness.

The advocate depute also did not ask her initial question in a loud, clear voice, but did so only when repeating the question and whilst directly facing the defence witness full on.

At this point it became clear that she was deliberately doing this to prompt the defence witness into having to ask her to repeat the question.

Suddenly the advocate depute stopped her line of enquiry and, staring directly at the defence witness, asked her to confirm again for the court her expert qualifications.

'I'm a forensic psychologist, a clinical psychologist, a member of the Fellowship of Psychology . . .' etc., etc.

'Thank you for reminding the court of your very impressive array of expert qualifications, Doctor. Most impressive indeed! Now, could you please tell the court how you would scale your individual performance in the question-and-answer session we have just completed, taking into consideration the fact that I've asked you several questions similar to those asked of the witnesses – who have notable learning difficulties – by the Crown prosecution psychologist, and that out of the ten asked of you, I've had to repeat at least seven of them? Now, Doctor, having previously stated your qualifications to the court, it is obvious that you don't possess a learning disability to submit as an excuse for not understanding my specific, but simple, questions first time around!'

The doctor tried to qualify her responses. 'But I didn't hear your questions clearly so therefore I had difficulty in understanding them properly!' she said.

The advocate depute paused for a second while focusing on the defence witness and then replied, 'Exactly, Doctor! Therefore when you asked me to repeat the question, it was to understand it and not to prompt you to give me a different answer!'

Then, turning to address the jury, knowing she had scored a point with her cross-examination, she said, 'I have no more questions for this expert witness!' before returning to her seat in the court.

It was a pleasure to be present during some expert and extremely clever questioning by the Crown prosecution!

That was a great court case!

Credit Fraud
• • •

An accused man appeared in court for credit card fraud.

Having been found guilty, he received a hefty fine from the sheriff.

The defence agent turned to his client and asked him how he would like to pay.

To which he confidently replied, 'American Express!'

Dr White at your Disposal

• • •

Whilst on duty one night in the station, the front door burst open and in ran a man in his mid-twenties who was a known troublemaker in the area.

He was bleeding profusely from a deep laceration to his chin, the type commonly referred to as a 'Kirk Douglas'!

He was screaming frantically, 'Help me! I'm getting chased wi' a team and they're tooled-up wi' blades!'

I then heard a loud disturbance outside and I saw about eight youths staring down from the pavement above, armed with knives and clubs.

On seeing me lift the radio to call for assistance, they all ran off.

My next priority was to try and stem the bleeding from his serious facial injury and summon an ambulance.

Using paper towels and applying pressure to the wound, I was able to stem the flow of blood. I searched through the office first-aid kit, but the items inside were so old they would not be out of place on the *Antiques Roadshow*!

The sterile pads would've given him gangrene!!

At this point I noticed on the wall of the female officers' toilet a Dr White's sanitary towel machine.

Now they're most definitely sterile!!

Out of sight of the young hard-man victim, I quickly ripped open the small package and removed the sanitary towel, which was about four inches long with a loop at either end.

Removing the sodden paper towels from his face, I replaced them with the sanitary towel, covering the wound and hooking the loops over his ears to hold it in place. (Why loops I'll never know. But I'll accept explanations on a stamped addressed envelope. From women only!)

I then told him to apply pressure to it.

He sat quietly, waiting for the ambulance, totally unaware of what the sterile dressing on his chin was.

That was, however, until four of my colleagues arrived at the office in response to my call for assistance.

They all instantly recognised the victim, who was sitting quietly feeling sorry for himself with his hammock dressing dangling from his ears.

That was it – they just couldn't contain themselves as they all fell about laughing and making trivial excuses in order to leave the office.

A few minutes later the ambulance arrived and, after a few titters from the paramedic crew, they soon removed the injured man, complete with sanitary towel, to the local accident and emergency department.

After they had left, as you would imagine, there was the usual 'period' of sick jokes from the cops who were present.

Particularly as this was the beginning of the 'festive period'.

Lucky Me
• • •

During an Old Firm match in Glasgow, a drunken fan was shouting and gesticulating abuse at my colleague and me. When we went towards him, he ran off across the busy main road without looking and was promptly blootered by a bus.

As I went to his assistance, he looked up at me, unfazed, and said, 'Wiz Ah no' lucky I didnae hurt myself there?'

'Not really, son,' I replied as we nicked him!

The Adventures of Harry the Polis

Sick Joke

. . .

Whilst on motorcycle patrol duties, I was involved in a road accident in the city centre of Glasgow.

A big orange and green Corporation double-decker bus collided with me head on. (Don't laugh – that bit was true!)

Anyway, I was knocked unconscious and rushed by ambulance to accident and emergency, where I was admitted to an observation ward.

Several hours later I regained consciousness and tried to focus my eyes.

I looked to my right and John Wayne appeared to be in the hospital bed next to me.

I then looked to my left and Clint Eastwood was in the other one.

Rubbing my eyes frantically, I called for the nurse and said, 'Where am I? Where am I?'

To which the nurse replied, 'You're in the Western!!' (Infirmary.)

No Change

...

During the old City of Glasgow police days, when wages were poor, the cops relied on shops and companies giving a 'discount' to police officers.

We would also get the odd steak pie, six rolls, pint of milk or apple tart handed in to the station by delivery van drivers.

Amalgamation came upon us and in 1975 we were united with cops from the Paisley area, who were slightly naive as to these practices.

During one nightshift, a county sergeant was partnering one of the Glasgow cops.

About five in the morning, the Glasgow cop was driving the patrol car when he suddenly sped off along the road after a bread van.

Once alongside it, he activated his blue lights and signalled the van driver to pull over and stop.

He then informed the sergeant to remain in the car while he spoke with the driver.

Having spoken to the driver, he then accompanied him to the back of the bread van. Within a few moments the cop returned to the police car carrying a loaf of bread, which he placed on the rear seat before driving away.

A few minutes later, the sergeant asked the Glasgow cop, 'What was that all about?'

He then explained that you would signal the van driver to pull into the side and stop. Then you would go up to him and ask to buy a loaf of bread – the driver would be so relieved to know that he was not being booked that he would duly oblige.

You would then offer the driver the money (28 pence) to

pay for the bread, which he would refuse to accept, saying, 'It's only a loaf, mate. I'll not miss one!'

You would then thank him and leave with your loaf.

Intrigued by the action of his fellow officer, the sergeant told the Glasgow cop that he would like to try it.

About fifteen minutes later, they drove along the road and saw another bread van.

They immediately sprung into action and pulled up alongside the van. With the blue lights flashing, they signalled the driver to pull over and stop.

As he pulled over, the sergeant told the Glasgow cop to stay in the patrol car and let him try it out for himself.

Up to the driver's window he went and within seconds, he was walking with the driver to the back of the van.

They were out of sight for a few moments before the sergeant appeared in the rear-view mirror, walking towards the police car, carrying four loaves of bread!

He then opened the back door and placed the loaves on the seat.

As he got back into the police car, the cop remarked, 'Four loaves, Sarge? You're being a bit greedy there.'

To which the sergeant replied sheepishly, 'Not really – he didn't have change of a pound!!'

Signing Session

· · ·

In possession of an arrest warrant for Tommy Morrison, I called at his last known home address.

Due to his record of violent behaviour towards the police, three other officers accompanied me.

After checking with the nameplates on each door in the tenement close, I made enquiries with a few of the tenants as to Tommy Morrison's whereabouts but to no avail. Not known at this address!

A few days later I was working in the office when two detectives from the Scottish Crime Squad called with an inquiry in the area.

They told me that they had called at the home of Morrison and cited the same address as the one I possessed for Tommy.

We realised that we were both interested in the same person, but they had just come from his house where they had obtained a written witness statement from him with regards to their inquiry.

I checked the address they had for him and it turned out he was staying 'care of' his girlfriend, with her name, Galvin, on the nameplate on the front door.

The detectives had taken all his relevant particulars, including his home telephone number.

I called the number, which was answered by his girl-friend, and I told her I was one of the officers of the Scottish Crime Squad who had called at her house to speak with Tommy. I explained that I had forgotten to have him sign his statement and asked if he could possibly call within the next half-hour at the local police station and do so.

The detectives sat quietly looking on with interest as I called their witness with this excuse, but after a few minutes they saw the funny side and couldn't contain themselves.

As they left the station, they insisted I call them and let them know the outcome.

Sure enough, within half an hour the door of the station opened and in walked Tommy Morrison.

'Hello, mate. I'm here to sign a statement for the Scottish Crime Squad,' he said assuredly.

'Oh, right. Can you just confirm your name and date of birth for me, please?' I asked him.

He quickly reeled off, 'Thomas Morrison, date of birth, twenty-fifth of October 1958.'

'That's what it says here, Tommy. You're the man I'm wanting!' I said.

I then walked around to the side door of the front desk and, opening it up, I invited him inside.

As we entered the office, I led him through to the detention room, where I opened the door.

He confidently entered the detention cell, totally unaware of where he was going.

Once he was safely inside, I locked the door behind him.

I then took great satisfaction in telling him, 'As Jeremy Beadle would say, Tommy, you've been framed!'

And all performed by yours truly with the minimum of fuss!

Disposing of Evidence

• • •

George Cowley was a cop from the East End of Glasgow, working out of the old Tobago Street station.

His pet hate was the scrap metal men, the guys who went about the streets uplifting old bits of cars, washing machines, copper piping – anything that earned them some beer money.

George was always stopping them and checking out their vehicles, looking for defects.

One day, George was just leaving the station when he saw 'Tank' Irwin, the Del Boy Trotter of Bridgeton, coming down the street towards him in his pick-up truck, fully laden with scrap metal.

George stepped out into the middle of the road and signalled for Tank to pull over and stop.

'Right, Mr Irwin, let's just check your vehicle for any defects!' said George, as he began to examine the pick-up for faults.

At this point Tank, a likeable rogue, got out and began to follow George around on his inspection of the vehicle.

'I don't think you'll find anything, Mr Cowley. I've just put it through an MOT,' said a confident Tank.

'Well, we'll see,' replied George as he continued with his thorough examination.

They arrived back at the front of the vehicle, but George was unable to detect any obvious faults.

He began lecturing Tank prior to letting him go on his way.

Just at that moment, George's eyes lit up.

'Got you!' he cried ecstatically.

He then put his hand through the open window and

removed the road tax disc from the windscreen and, on examining it very carefully, he cried out, 'Ya beauty! I've got you! Fraudulent display of tax disc!'

George could hardly contain himself as he jigged about the footpath in complete and total ecstasy, performing a dance routine that Michael Flatley would have been proud of.

While George did his victory celebration, Tank remained very calm and collected as he watched. Then he said, 'Can I see the tax disc, please, Mr Cowley?'

Not thinking about the consequences of his actions, George handed the fraudulent disc over to Tank who, without the slightest hesitation, crumpled it up into a ball and stuffed it into his mouth.

As his evidence was being chewed before his very eyes, George jumped on to Tank's back and placed his hands around his neck to try and stop him swallowing the evidence.

On seeing what appeared to be an unprovoked physical attack by George on Tank, some of the other cops, coming out of the station, ran over and pulled George off and away from Tank in order to restrain him.

This was all the time Tank required and, with one final gulp, he had disposed of the entire evidence.

The Ballad of Big Bad Alec

...

Big Alec MacLellan was a gentle giant who was responsible for the running of the police motor vehicle pound.

He was the guy you went to see about getting your car back after it had been towed away by the polis, because it would end up in his vehicle pound.

He was a character in the force and a legend in his own mind.

This poem was written to celebrate his retirement in 1982.

There was a big polis called Alec, custodier of the police vehicle pound.

When customers called at his office, they could never find Alec around.

There would often appear a wee notice which plainly in pencil did say,

'I'll only be out for a minute,' but he really meant 'all bloody day'.

I suppose he's gone out to the pub – Maxwell's or maybe McNee's.

It was heard from one of his colleagues, 'He'll drink till he lands on his knees.'

His last trip was out to the bookies. He walked from the pound in a dream.

He ended up in the chemists and asked them for vanishing cream!

No Hiding Place

· · ·

In possession of an arrest warrant, I called at the home address of the named accused and knocked on his door. After a moment, his wife answered.

I told her why I was there and she swore to me, hand on heart, that Joe was not in the house and hadn't stayed there for some time.

She also stated that she was unaware of his present whereabouts.

I asked if I could make a customary search of the house in order to satisfy myself and also to confirm her story.

She reluctantly agreed to my request.

I searched the house, which was also occupied by several of her children, all under the age of five. I was about to leave when the wife stopped me in the hallway and said she would contact me immediately should he return home.

At this point my attention was drawn to one of the small children, standing in a bedroom.

I looked through the hinge opening of the door.

To my surprise, she was facing a double wardrobe and saying, 'Dadda! Dadda!'

She was also stretching her hands up towards the door.

I continued to watch her for a moment, when suddenly a hand appeared from inside the wardrobe and began waving the child away.

The hand then disappeared back inside.

Desperately trying not to laugh, I entered the room, knocked on the wardrobe door and said, 'Knock knock, Dadda! Guess who's here to see you!'

The accused fell out the wardrobe, laughing uncontrollably, and said, 'See weans! Don't ye just love them?'

No Armchair Stampede

...

There had been an incident at the rear of Celtic Football Park whereby it was alleged that Strathclyde Police mounted officers had stampeded, on horseback, football supporters who had congregated in Janefield Street.

The sensitive inquiry was being dealt with by one of our most senior and respected officers, Chief Superintendent John T. Dickson.

During this ongoing inquiry, there was an international football match coming up between Scotland and England at Hampden Park and I was trying to get tickets.

One day I was called into Superintendent Irwin's office. He said to me, 'I've to ask you, Harry, are you still looking for tickets for the big game? If so, Mr Dickson has two for sale.'

I told him yes, I was still looking for tickets. He called Mr Dickson at his office in Pitt Steet HQ to let him know.

'Right, Harry!' said the superintendent. 'You've to go up to his office right now!'

I went straight to HQ and knocked on the chief superintendent's office door.

'In you come, Harry!' he said. He opened a drawer, took out the match tickets and handed them to me.

'Nowadays I prefer to watch the game in the comfort of my armchair in the house,' he said convincingly.

To which I replied, jokingly of course, 'Well, let's be honest, sir, you've less chance of getting trampled by a big bloody polis horse!'

Needless to say he was not amused by my comment.

But I bet he had a right good chuckle after I left his office!

A Clash of Personalities

· · ·

I was summoned to the chief inspector's office for my appraisal/assessment, commonly referred to as your MOT.

Halfway through the appraisal report, the chief inspector said, 'I detect from some of the remarks made by your shift sergeant that you don't get on with him.'

'I think that's a fair observation,' I replied.

'What appears to be the problem?' he asked me.

'It's just a clash of personalities, sir,' I said. 'He doesn't have one.'

'A personality clash? Do you think a change of shift would help?'

Whereupon I replied with a straight face, 'Frankly, no, sir! I don't think he could get on with anybody!'

Hearing Things

· · ·

A ned in the court was being sentenced for his offence.

'Have you anything you would like to say?' asked the sheriff.

The accused replied rather despondently, 'Fuck all!'

The sheriff called out to the procurator fiscal, 'What did he just say there?'

' "Fuck all," m'lord!' replied the fiscal.

To which the sheriff said, 'I'm sure I heard him say something!'

Don't Blow a Fuse

· · ·

One day my partner O'Reilly arrived at the station in his new car, a second-hand Hillman Avenger.

Proud as punch he was as he led me on an inspection of it.

There were the statutory furry dice hanging from the interior mirror and stuck on either side of the front windscreen were 'Eddie' and 'Mary' – very impressive – and the wee dog with the bobbing head in the rear window shelf. A classic!

On the dashboard he had fitted an impressive array of a dozen coloured switches on to a velvet-covered dashboard extension which protruded out from the original Hillman dashboard. It was like a pilot's cockpit!

He could not contain his obvious enthusiasm as he gave me a demonstration of the changes he had made, showing me all the extra switches and what they did.

'This one operates new fog lights at the front and this one operates new lights at the rear!' He continued, 'This one is high-intensity lights I've fitted and this switch here operates a quadraphonic stereo music system!'

He then flicked the switch down and out blasted a David Bowie song. 'And this one—'

At this point, I interrupted him as smoke began belching out from behind his new 'switch' dashboard.

'I take it this one operates a getaway smokescreen, or is it a direct line to the local fire station?'

O'Reilly looked on in disbelief. 'Shit! The wiring system's faulty!' he replied, panicking. 'Quick, Harry, get a fire extinguisher!'

'What switch should I press for that, then?' I asked, while trying to remain calm.

Within five minutes, O'Reilly's pride and joy was reduced to 'Ashes to Ashes'!!

And O'Reilly was left 'Aladdin Sane'!!

The Music of Life

· · ·

The police were attending a call regarding the suicide of a man in a tenement building.

Whilst awaiting the arrival of the casualty surgeon and staff from the city mortuary, a neighbour appeared at her door and enquired, 'What's the matter, Constable?'

'It's your neighbour, hen – he's committed suicide!' replied the officer.

The shocked woman gasped in horror. 'How did he do it?' she asked, deeply concerned.

'He hung himself last night!' responded the officer.

The woman paused for a moment, before turning around to her son, who was standing just inside the door, and saying, 'Here, I hope you weren't playing that bloody Bob Dylan again!'

Funny Text from a Friend

· · ·

My missus came out of the shower one morning and stood naked in front of the bedroom mirror, looking at herself.

She said, 'My eyes are baggy, my tits are sagging and I look horribly fat and ugly! Pay me a compliment, darling!'

To which I replied, 'OK – your eyesight's fuckin' spot on!'

I Never Parked It Like That

. . .

Colin Muir was a very laid-back cop whom I worked with for a short time as a young probationer.

His nickname amongst the local neds was 'Gallus' owing to his laid-back attitude and the way he reacted when dealing with them.

He also loved himself to bits and fancied himself as a charmer.

One night we received a call to attend a disturbance at a wedding reception at the Pollokshaws Burgh Halls, caused by local gatecrashers!

On our arrival we parked and locked the panda outside the main door and entered the hall to deal with the complaint.

There was a large crowd in the hallway that dispersed sharpish on seeing us enter the main reception hall.

'Right, what's the problem, my man?' Gallus asked one of the guests.

That was the signal for the entire wedding party to try and all speak at the one time.

'Woh, woh, woh! Cool the beans! Now, what about you, sweetheart – can you tell me what happened?' said Gallus as he pointed to a rather pretty young woman, taking hold of her arm and leading her to one side.

During the conversation that followed, Gallus spent more time chatting up his handpicked witness, noting her name, address and telephone number.

While this was taking place, the elderly hall keeper tried several times to interrupt Gallus – in full flow – but Gallus repeatedly told him not to interrupt and to wait his turn.

Finally Gallus walked over to the stage and interrupted the wedding band in the middle of their performance of

'You're the One that I Want' and took the microphone off the singer.

All the while, I stood there, being the boy, quietly cringing with embarrassment at the unbelievable way he was dealing with this complaint.

He then assured the entire wedding party, using the microphone, that he was the local sheriff and this was his area and all the neds feared him.

Now that he had made a personal appearance at the wedding reception, they would be too frightened to return because, more than anything, they wouldn't want to upset him.

He finished off like a master of ceremonies by announcing, 'I want you all to enjoy the rest of your night, especially John and Morag, the happy couple.'

He then led the wedding party with a toast to the happy couple before handing the microphone back to the band singer.

I couldn't believe it when the wedding party, table after table, stood up and applauded him.

Some of the guests even held out their hands to shake his and a few of the ladies even kissed him as he left the hall, waving them goodbye.

Out in the hallway, the elderly hall keeper was still waiting to speak with him.

'Right, my man, what's your problem, then?' asked a confident Gallus.

The old hall keeper said, 'I don't have one, sir, but I think you do! Look!'

He then ushered us to the main door of the hall where – to the total embarrassment and humiliation of Gallus and, I must admit, the complete and total amusement of the old hall keeper and myself – the neds, on their way out, had overturned our panda car on to its roof.

Ladies and
Gentlemen – Ben Doon
· · ·

Whilst a member of the Police Social Committee, it was my duty from time to time to act as the master of ceremonies at cabaret functions.

I had always managed to avoid it but, with the absence of some of the other members, I was nominated to take my turn.

The star of the cabaret was a very funny comedian called Ben Gunn, whom I was introduced to on his arrival at the club.

He gave me this spiel that he wanted me to say when I introduced him, about how he had just returned from a very successful tour of America and was now appearing at the top of the bill on the Sydney Devine Silver Jubilee Show at the Pavilion Theatre in Glasgow.

'After the performance,' he said, 'we'll have a drink!'

Now, earlier in the evening this would not have been a problem but, after several large Whyte & Mackay whiskies, the art of breathing was becoming a big problem for me.

It came to the penultimate act, a Caribbean steel band dressed in bright orange shirts. They looked like they had all been Tangoed as they played their big oil drums.

By the way, the nearest they came to the Caribbean was in a holiday brochure – I knew three out of the four of them personally, having recognised them as drivers on the Corporation buses, working out of the Larkfield bus garage.

With the previous turn, a country and western act called the Pheasant Pluckers, I had developed dyslexia and read their introduction wrong, referring to them as some 'C***s with vests on' and 'They're the Pleasant F***ers.'

The other committee members were telling me, 'Right, Harry, we think you got away with that one,' but not to make any mistakes with the introduction of Ben!

I jumped on to the stage with my microphone and said confidently, 'Let's hear it one more time – all the way from Jamaica (Street), the Caribbean Steel Band!'

The audience applauded enthusiastically.

As the applause died down I said, 'They rejected an engagement to go on a worldwide tour. Apparently two of the band members wanted to go somewhere else! I'm also informed that the boys want me to tell you they're sorry there will be no encores as there's a shortage of bus drivers tonight and they've all got to report for double shifts!'

I continued in this vein, getting carried away with myself, leaning on the microphone stand like a real pro.

'Two of the band members are actual twins! They used to be triplets but they ate the other brother between them one night! In true conundrum fashion, he was ate before he was seven! Now, we have come to the star of our show, an act that has been thrown off more stages than big John Wayne! In fact, he tells me he is just back from America where he underwent a nose transplant but, unfortunately, his finger rejected it!'

Suddenly, through the smoky haze I could see some of the committee members making their way down the sides of the hall, trying not to draw too much attention to themselves, but I was on a roll and wasn't going to get off the stage that easily, so I continued, 'He was telling me earlier that while he was in America for three weeks, he lost nine stone of ugly fat – apparently he got a quickie divorce!'

That was the last straw – one of the committee had the other end of the microphone and was pulling and tugging it, so in order to prevent any further embarrassment, I quickly announced, 'So will you please put your hands together and give a big Lochinch police club welcome to the one and only Mr Ben Doon!! Hic!'

Ben was not one bit amused at my introduction. He took the mike off me and called me a frustrated comedian.

He then did his performance, cutting his act short by twenty minutes, and promptly left the club.

Needless to say I was never again asked to perform as the MC at a police social club!! Although I did apologise to Ben when we met on another occasion! I think he still held a grudge!!

Grass is Grass
. . .

A professional footballer was arrested for possession of cannabis.

The young arresting cop, on recognising him as a sportsman, asked, 'What's the best, grass or AstroTurf?'

To which the footballer replied, 'I don't know – I've never smoked AstroTurf!'

Bombs Away

· · ·

In the late seventies and early eighties we were receiving numerous bomb alerts – all false alarms, except for one night when I received a call to attend a well-known Irish pub in the Gorbals.

While en route I received another call, confirming it as a genuine bomb gone off!

Within several minutes I arrived at the locus to find the entire area swamped with police personnel.

Fortunately no one was seriously injured.

I left after a short time and was instructed to return to my station and see the patrol inspector.

Now this patrol inspector was nicknamed 'the Olympic Flame' because he never went out!

On my return, he wanted to be fully appraised of the situation.

Keeping a straight face, I began, 'Right, allegedly a man wearing a Rangers scarf entered the pub and walked up to the barman and asked for three bottles of Bell's whisky, four bottles of Smirnoff vodka, three bottles of Gordon's gin, two dozen cans of Tennent's lager, two dozen cans of McEwan's Pale Ale and four dozen cans of McEwan's Export. At this point the barman interrupted him and said, "Excuse me, but this is going to cost you a bomb!"

'The man took an object out of his jacket pocket, threw it towards the barman and said, "There you are – you have two minutes."'

The Flame looked puzzled, laughed nervously then asked, 'Is that true?'

Harry the Unknown Osmond

• • •

I shall now reveal a hidden talent and long-time secret of mine.

Back in the early seventies, the Apollo Theatre in Glasgow was a very popular venue for all the big music acts – Status Quo, Thin Lizzy, Dr Hook, the Osmonds . . .

During this time I had the good fortune to work at one of the Osmond brothers' concerts. I was also quite friendly with Jan, the manager of the Apollo at the time.

Whilst on duty, I asked Jan if he could get me a souvenir or autograph from the band for my young sister Kim, who was about twelve years old and a really big fan.

Jan said he would see what he could do for me.

A short time later, Jan called me over and said he had managed to secure an autographed copy of their album *The Plan*, which he would keep in his office until after the concert.

I was over the moon and couldn't contain my excitement, so I telephoned my mother to let Kim know what I had for her.

After the Osmonds and the screaming teenage girl audience had all but gone, I went to Jan's office to collect my prized possession.

To my complete and utter disappointment, Jan informed me that during the concert a thief entered his office and had stolen various items, the autographed album included.

I was devastated at this news.

What was I going to do? I had promised my little sister an autographed Osmonds album.

Fortunately Jan came to the rescue with another Osmonds album, minus the autographs of one of the biggest and most popular bands in the world.

What was I going to do? Simple! I signed the autographs of Donny, Merrill and Jay!

As for the rest of the brothers . . . well, that was my colleagues accompanying me on the night.

I'll spare the blushes of who were little Jimmy and Marie!

So, Kim, who treasured her copy of *The Plan* for all these years – the secret's out. Your big brother Harry was Donny Osmond!

'And they called it puppy lov—'

'Shuut uupp!'

'Oops! Sorry, pet!'

Guess Who?

· · ·

Imagine working for a company with slightly more than 500 employees which has the following statistics:

Twenty-nine have been accused of wife abuse, 7 have been arrested for fraud, 19 have been accused of writing bad cheques, 119 have directly or indirectly been responsible for bankrupting at least 3 businesses, 3 have been convicted for assault, 70 have been refused credit cards due to bad debt, 14 have been arrested on drug-related charges, 8 have been imprisoned for theft by shoplifting, 20 are currently defendants in criminal lawsuits and, in the last year, 83 have been arrested for drunk driving.

Can you guess what the organisation is?

It's the 535 members of the United States Congress! The same people who implement hundreds of new laws each year.

Makes you wonder how the British Government would fare.

To Hell with Tulliallan

While attending the Tulliallan Police College for my three-month probationer training spell, I was taking part in a football tournament.

Several teams were made up from the large contingent of probationer students.

My team had qualified for the second round and I was supporting my mate, Jimmy Clark, playing for his team in the hope that he would also qualify.

Unbeknown to me, also present as a spectator at the rear of the hall was none other than the director of junior training – or DJT as he was better known – and Inspector John Elliot, head of the junior training instructors.

During the game, Jimmy had the ball at his feet, beat two defenders and, with only the goalkeeper in front of him, missed and knocked the ball wide of the post.

'Jesus Christ!' I shouted in sheer frustration.

At this blasphemous outburst, the DJT asked Inspector Elliot, 'Who shouted that?'

The inspector called to me, 'Was that you, Mr Morris?'

'Yes, sir!' I replied, annoyed at myself for the outburst.

'You'll go to hell for that, Morris!' he said.

To which I responded in a jocular manner, 'With all due respect, sir, I've been here for two months and three weeks!' That raised a laugh from the students!

Later the same day, I was called up to the DJT's office and disciplined for my remarks and warned regarding my future conduct.

How trivial!!

Anti-Abortion Demo

. . .

I was on duty at a large public demonstration (yes – another demonstration in Scotland) by a group of anti-abortionists!

It was a beautiful bright sunny day in Glasgow and they were marching all the way from Blythswood Square to Glasgow Green in the East End of the city.

My attention was drawn to the 2,500 or so demonstrators and wondering how I could divide them up into five sections, which were the following.

One fifth of the demonstrators were men! C'mon, guys!

The second fifth was made up of children, and most of them had an awful lot of growing up to do before they needed to worry about abortions.

My third section was made up of nuns! I'm saying absolutely nothing because I respect their total commitment to the Church.

The fourth section was made from old-age pensioners. Now let's face it, there's virtually no chance, unless you're Sophia Loren, of ever getting pregnant at their age, so what have they got to be worried about?

Which brings me to my last section, which was made up with heavily pregnant mothers-to-be. Most of them, by the end of the march, were so exhausted and totally exasperated with the heat, coupled with the constant greeting, moaning and complaining of their own children and those belonging to the other demonstrators, that several had already changed their opinions and were now definitely for it.

The following week there was a pro-abortion demonstration and I'm positive I recognised several familiar faces!

What Are You Doing?

. . .

I called at the local police station and entered the radio control room. I asked a female civilian computer operator to check the registration number of a suspected stolen car.

The assistant was about to drink a cup of coffee at the time but she agreed to my request.

While she was entering the details of the car, I lit up a cigarette and hovered behind her, leaning over her shoulder.

I saw out of the corner of my eye what appeared to be a round ashtray, to my right-hand side.

Still looking at the computer screen, I reached over and began to stub out my cigarette butt!

After three or four attempts to put my cigarette out, I looked over towards the ashtray and, to my horror, discovered what turned out to be her Wagon Wheel chocolate biscuit!

Frantically I began to try and discreetly wipe off the ash and return the biscuit to its original appearance and appetising best, but the computer operator turned around and caught me in the act.

Over the years that followed, I presented her with numerous packets of biscuits but I don't think she ever forgave me for what I did with her smoky Wagon Wheel!

Mind you, I just might have created a new Wagon Wheel flavour!

By the way, Cathy, I also stopped smoking shortly after this!

The Court Jester

. . .

I was working at the High Court in Glasgow along with several other cops as part of the courts branch.

Whilst I was sitting in the police control room with Wee Hughie Dewar, the cop who operated the security gates and surveillance cameras, I was going through some of my voice impersonations with Hughie and we were having a good laugh.

Five out of the six courts were finished for the day and the cops who were working in them were all sitting about the police common room, quietly reading a newspaper or playing cards to kill time until they received permission to go home.

This was the normal practice and I found it extremely boring sitting about, so Hughie suggested I telephone the duty officer, whose room was directly opposite our position and who was responsible for the officers employed in the courts.

I would then impersonate the courts branch inspector and we would observe his reaction from the window of our room.

I rang his telephone and watched as he answered it. I then said, 'Hello, Paul. Inspector Harrison here. Has anybody been looking for me?'

'Yes, sir!' Paul replied. 'Mr Martin was looking for you.'

'OK, I'll give him a call!' I said. 'What's happening elsewhere with the courts, then?' I continued, aware that all but one of the courts were finished for the day.

'All my courts are finished for the day, bar one!' he replied immediately.

'Are the cops all sitting about in the common room then?' I enquired.

'Yes, sir. Do you want me to give them something to do here or should I send them all over to the Sheriff Court to work?' asked Paul.

'No, don't bother. Just send them all home – they've worked hard today and deserve a break!' I replied rather convincingly.

'OK, sir, you're the boss!' he said.

I then put the phone down and Hughie and I had a right good laugh at Paul's expense.

Suddenly my facial expression changed as I looked up along the cell passage corridor and saw all the cops from the common room, with their civilian jackets on and carrying their bags, walking towards me.

I quickly ran into Paul's room and informed him it hadn't been the inspector calling, it had been me doing an impersonation of him.

To which he said, 'Well, Harry boy, you better do another one and explain to this lot coming down the corridor – I don't think they'll be very happy with you!'

I then ran out to meet them and, casually putting my hands up to stop them, I said, 'Sorry, guys, you've got to go back to the common room. Paul was just winding you all up. He's sitting in his office laughing away, the lousy bugger!

This news was greeted by groans from the disgruntled cops, who were very annoyed with Paul for his sick joke.

I managed, in my own inimitable way, to alleviate the situation and pass the buck on to the unsuspecting Paul at the same time!

Relief, for My Relief

. . .

At the end of a shift, I was going to a friend's house to view a live boxing match. I had arranged for another friend to call at the police station at the end of my duties so that we could share a taxi.

Now my friend Brad is a six-feet-plus black guy who just happens to be a deaf mute!

He duly arrived at the agreed time and I informed him, using sign language, that I was just awaiting my relief station officer arriving before I could leave and that, in the meantime, he should just wait in the front office area!

Brad decided to look at the posters on the wall and, after several minutes, the front door to the station opened.

Brad immediately felt the draught from the door on his neck and turned around to face it, as in walked Donnie, my relief officer.

With Donnie looking at me and Brad with his back to me, looking at Donnie, I spoke in a loud voice and said, 'For the last time, sir, there is only one officer working in this station called Donnie and I can assure you he hasn't been sleeping with your wife and daughter. Now will you fuck off out of the police station!'

All the time I was talking, Brad had his back to me, staring at Donnie, who had frozen in his tracks and was staring back at Brad, with what can only be described as a look of total shock on a face that now lacked any colour.

Everything stopped for a moment while Donnie suffered in silence, then I allowed a huge grin to cover my face and said, 'Don't look so worried, Donnie, I'm only joking. He can't hear a word – he's totally deaf!'

At which point Donnie heaved a huge sigh of relief before scurrying off to the toilet to relieve himself! No doubt!

0 to 60 in Seconds

· · ·

During the miners' strike and subsequent picket lines at Bilston Colliery, a young police probationer was on picket-line duty, where officers were pushed, jostled, spat upon and struck with missiles thrown at them by the crowd.

The young probationer finally snapped, unable to stand the abuse any more. He broke ranks and ran off, screaming at the top of his voice, 'I can't take any more! I can't take any more!'

He ran as fast as he could, covering a distance of several hundred metres before he eventually stumbled and fell over.

As he lay on the ground, with his head in his hands, sobbing uncontrollably, he heard a deep husky voice say, 'Get a grip of yourself, lad!'

Looking over in the direction of the voice, he saw a pair of highly polished black shoes.

'I'm so sorry, Sergeant!' he blurted out.

The voice replied rather indignantly, 'Who are you calling sergeant? I'm your superintendent!'

To which the young probationer replied, 'Fuck me! Did I run that far?'

The Demolition Man

. . .

One evening I received a call from my 'faither' in the polis, Willie Craig, the duty officer of the force control room.

Willie wanted me to assist a distressed woman who was locked out of her house and calling from a nearby telephone kiosk.

I attended immediately and after I had comforted the upset woman, she explained that she had been out with her husband and another couple for a meal and a drink.

During the evening, her husband had complained of feeling unwell and had decided to go home early, leaving her and the other couple to enjoy the rest of the night.

On arriving home later, she was unable to gain access to her house because her husband's house key was still in the lock inside.

She stated that she had knocked on the door for some time and, getting no response, had tried telephoning the house for almost thirty minutes, but there had been no answer. She was now becoming increasingly concerned about her husband.

I followed the distressed woman to her front door, which was on the first floor of a red sandstone tenement building.

The exterior house door was solid and had been decorated with mahogany wood grain panelled plywood.

The fitted door facing was made of a fancy ogee design and was finished off with imitation wrought-iron hinges, door knocker, letter box, nameplate and door handle. All very nice and decorative.

Above the door was a large, colourful stained-glass window.

Having tried initially to force the door with the minimum of force, the job called for more force to be used – the Doc Marten boot!

I had several attempts at kicking the door but to no avail – all I succeeded in doing was bursting the decorative mahogany panelling on the door.

I also, due to the extreme force I was using, managed to crack the shiny gold nameplate.

I made my apologies to the sobbing woman, who waved them away, being more concerned with her husband and his state of health.

Change of plan!

I then tried, with the use of a large screwdriver, to remove the fancy ogee door facing in order to gain access to the door lock.

All was going well until halfway down the facing – 'Snap!' – the facing broke off.

I turned around to look at the woman, standing watching with a paper tissue in her face, drying her tears as I systematically demolished her door in instalments.

'Oh, just carry on and get me in!' she said.

I then proceeded to rip the rest of the facing off the door and, with the aid of the large screwdriver, chipped away at the door standard to try and expose the mortice lock.

With no luck there either, I returned to kicking the now almost demolished and unrecognisable fancy panelled door!

With all the noise coming from my eager attempts to gain entry, a neighbour from across the landing opened his door and, on seeing the plight I was facing, suggested, 'Why don't you just smash the window above the door and gain entry that way?'

At which point the sobbing woman, still breaking her heart, shrieked at him, 'Why don't you just fuck right off! Don't you think he's done enough bloody damage to my door?'

Then realising what she had said in her outburst, she looked around at me and said, 'Oh, I'm sorry, officer. I know you mean well!'

She had just finished her apology when – 'click!'

We all turned around as the door was opened and a very sleepy-looking man was standing there, dressed in vest and pants.

'What's all the racket?' he asked, completely unaware of all that had occurred. 'What have you done, hen?'

The sobbing woman's facial expression changed as she charged at her husband, whom she had been so extremely worried about.

She began to scream hysterically at him, 'You dozy bastard, look what you've caused and there's nothing up wi' you!'

She then began to punch and kick him, as he tried to make his way along the hallway, out of her reach.

As for me! I didn't wait for her to thank me – I got off my mark quickly before she had another look at her door and took revenge on me!

The result of the call to the force control room was: 'Entry gained by the police. All in order. The female reporter wishes to thank the police for a job well done!' Then I added, 'And do we have the number of a good emergency joiner?'

The Glasgow Olympics

· · ·

A few years ago, whilst watching athletics on the television and the intense methods of preparation undertaken by some of the world's most notable athletes, it suddenly struck me the amount of preparation the everyday wee Glesca punter put into his!

By that I mean his 100 metres and 200 metres sprint races, his high jump, pole vault and long jump, etc.

You see, none of his athletic exploits are performed in such prestigious competitions, but rather the opposite. For example, if you resided in a Glasgow tenement-housing scheme, the following situation would arise regularly.

One minute you would be playing in a tough competitive game of rounders, street football or kick the can, when all of a sudden – panic!! You looked up and the polis would be plodding it out, coming down the street towards you.

Whoosh!! You were off, and I mean *off* – your legs were just a blur as they propelled you along at breakneck speed. (That's very, very fast, by the way.)

I would hurdle every obstacle in front of me, whether it was a 7-foot garden fence, an 8-foot boundary wall or a 12-foot opening over a stream, and any obstacle that I couldn't master, I would just run straight over or through.

Wood and brick debris would be brushed aside by my sheer speed and determination.

Linford Christie would have no chance. Nobody, but nobody was going to catch me!

Then suddenly, a strange but alarming thought struck me – what the hell am I running for?

I'm the *community police* for the area!

Parking Disability

. . .

There was a CID officer nicknamed 'Sven' because of his Scandinavian good looks, tanned skin and physical build.

Apart from his smart stylish suits and blond hair, he also drove about in a white sports car that suited his personality and stood out.

One day he went shopping with his girlfriend to the newly opened Parkhead Forge shopping centre.

Unable to find a parking space near the entrance, Sven decided to park his fancy new sports car in the only space available, a vacant disabled parking space.

Off they went, hand in hand, Sven turning his head back one last time to view his shining pride and joy parked safely in the car park.

After several hours spent accumulating bag after bag of groceries and clothing, it was time to leave the centre and return to the 'Svenmobile'.

They strolled along the mall, laden down with bags, heading for the exit doors, to the car park . . .

Sven's boyish smile changed to a look of shock as, to his horror, he saw his dream machine being lifted on to the rear of a Hiab recovery vehicle for removal to the police pound.

Standing alongside, taking notes, were two imposing leather-clad motorcycle cops.

Sven dropped his heavy grocery bags on the footpath and said to his girlfriend, 'Here, grab hold of that lot!'

Then, panic-stricken, he ran up to the cops and asked, 'What the hell are you doing? That's my car you're lifting!'

The cop who was writing vigorously in his notebook paused for a moment, looked over at Sven and said,

'You're parked illegally in a disabled parking bay, sir!' Then, looking Sven up and down, he added, 'You certainly don't look disabled to me!'

Sven thought for a moment as he stared at the cop then turned around to see his girlfriend bringing up the rear, carrying the heavy bags. He turned back to the cop and, pointing over at her, he said confidently, 'Well, does she look normal to you?'

They both looked over to see his slightly built girlfriend, laden down with all the heavy bags, shuffling along in high heels and struggling under her load.

The cop allowed himself a wry smile before continuing with his notes.

As for the girlfriend, on hearing Sven's discourteous remarks about her physical condition, she dropped the grocery bags where she stood and shouted at Sven, 'Is that right, ya big diddy! Well, ye can just carry the messages yersel', I'm out of here!' before storming away in a bad mood.

A hard and expensive lesson for Sven to learn, but if you are not disabled, don't park in the bay!

I'd Know Her Anywhere
• • •

A road accident resulted in a woman passenger being fatally injured.

The driver of the vehicle, who was unconscious, had suffered serious head injuries but was identified by one of the police officers present as David Green.

However, the problem arose as to the identity of the woman passenger.

On calling at David Green's relatives' address to inform them of his injuries, they were informed he had a long-term relationship with Maggie Reid, who was separated from her husband.

Several inquiries later, they called at the home address of Robert Reid (the husband) and informed him of the road accident and of their suspicion that the fatally injured woman could be his wife Maggie.

The husband was distraught at this news and sat down, breaking his heart, tears pouring from his eyes.

Big Davie, one of the officers present, gave him a glass of water and a cigarette, which he readily accepted, even though, he was later to admit, he had stopped smoking three weeks before.

The next task was to convey the distraught Mr Reid (several cigarettes later) to the city mortuary in Glasgow in order to identify the deceased woman.

At the mortuary the officers displayed their sensitive side to Mr Reid.

They told him that one side of her face had been badly injured and therefore, if he wished to, he could view the deceased on the mortuary video monitor.

Mr Reid declined their offer, saying he would rather see her up close himself.

As he entered the room, he broke down again in a flood of tears.

'That's her! It's her! Oh, my God, whit will I tell the weans? She's gone! Their mammy's gone for ever. Oh, God, I miss her already!'

Deeply distressed, Big Davie led Mister Reid back to the police car and returned him home to the comfort of his friends and family.

After noting the relevant particulars for his report, Big Davie and his partner returned to the police station several hours later.

As they entered the office, I said, 'What kept you two, then?'

Big Davie replied, 'What kept us? We've been here, there and every-bloody-where, trying to get the deceased woman identified!'

'And did you get her identified?' I asked.

'Eventually,' said Davie. 'It's Maggie Reid.'

'Maggie Reid?' I said, surprised, then shook my head. 'Don't think so, Davie.'

'It was, Harry!' said Big Davie. 'She's been identified!'

'Sorry, guys, you're wrong – Maggie Reid was in here only half an hour ago, asking how badly injured David Green was and, I might add, she looked very much alive and kicking!' I responded.

Big Davie and his partner looked at each other, puzzled! Then Davie asked me, 'Well, who's in the city mortuary? 'Cause Robert Reid was positive it was his missus lying there and even identified her.'

'Well, it wasn't his missus, it was "lucky" Jack Kelly's

daughter, Sandra,' I explained. 'The traffic cops have got the report to write – you must have just missed them at the city mortuary!'

Big Davie slumped down into an office chair.

'That bugger Robert Reid smoked about twelve of my fags. In fact, at one point he was that upset I was nearly greeting with him!'

His partner said, 'So much for his statement, "I'd know her anywhere!" And what about the bit where he said, "We had three lovely weans together." He must have been making love to her in the dark.'

'Crikey! He even cuddled her body and kissed her!' added Davie.

I then said, 'Well, he's in for a shock in the morning when Maggie knocks on his front door!'

To which Big Davie retorted, 'Having seen his reaction tonight, he'll probably no' recognise her!!'

Learn to Drive

• • •

One day while driving a traffic patrol car along the road, a black hackney carriage (that's a taxi to you) suddenly and without warning made a U-turn in the road in front of me, causing me to take evasive action to avoid a collision.

As I came to a stop, I leaned out of the driver's window and shouted at him, 'Where the hell did you learn to drive?'

To which the taxi driver shouted back, 'In the polis – I used to be a traffic cop with you, Harry, remember?'

I then recognised him and, sure enough, it was David Colvin — an ex-traffic cop!

The Adventures of Harry the Polis

. . .

Post-it Thru the Window

• • •

'Stinker' Smith was the policeman in charge of the temporary police station on Paisley Road in Glasgow, which was a Portakabin.

He was enjoying a game of cards during his tea break with some of the colleagues on his shift when someone entered the front office.

He put down his cards and went through to the front to see who it was.

There, standing holding an injured pigeon, was a small girl, who explained to Stinker how she had found it on the road outside.

Stinker took possession of the injured pigeon and said he would contact the local vet to mend its obviously broken wing.

He then went into his drawer and handed the small girl a sweet, thanking her for her kindness.

Stinker returned with the pigeon to the back office and, opening a hopper window, promptly threw it out.

He then sat back down to play his hand of cards.

Several minutes later, the front door opened again. Down went his cards for a second time and through he went to see who it was this time.

To his surprise, the same small girl was standing there, this time holding a tiny kitten!

'I found this little kitten outside on the footpath and I think it's lost its mummy!'

Reaching over to take possession of the kitten from her, he opened his drawer, handed her another sweet and said he would call the local cat and dog home to come and collect it. He also suggested that she make her way home before her mummy reported her missing!

He then rushed through to the rear of the office and just as before, he opened the hopper window and threw the kitten out.

He then sat back down to play his hand of cards.

His colleagues remarked on his lack of compassion, which he totally ignored.

Picking up his cards again, he continued with his game, when – you've guessed it! – the door to the front office was opened again.

Becoming exasperated by these untimely interruptions to his card game, Stinker slammed his cards down and said, 'If that's her again, I'm going to throw her out the window!'

He then rushed through to the front office, but to his surprise it was a workman standing with the office door half opened and holding the reins of a horse, pulling a cart.

'Can I help you, sir?' enquired Stinker.

'Yes, you can, mate!' replied the workman. 'I found this horse wandering about the road outside your office, with apparently no one in charge of it. It's going to cause an accident.'

Before Stinker could say a word, a voice called out from the rear of the office, 'Let's see you throw that out the window!' followed by loud hysterical laughter!!

The Lord Provost of Russia

· · ·

I had the good fortune to meet and strike up a friendship with the late David Hodge, former Lord Provost of Glasgow.

This is a story he related to me about a visit he made to the USSR.

'My visit was full of surprises and I found so much that was completely different to what I had been led to believe. The people were happier than I expected. It was interesting to attend church services and find standing room only.

'I had a memorable experience in Sochi, a delightful resort on the Black Sea, with a tropical climate and unending sunshine. Apparently some years ago a learned professor experimented with citrus fruits and he found that all fruits of this family could, by being grafted, grow together on one single tree. This actually happens in a garden of remembrance and distinguished visitors and Russians of note are invited to make a graft, usually a fruit native of their own country, and these are labelled.

'It was interesting to read the names of Uri Gargarin, Mrs Ghandi, presidents and ambassadors of most countries in the world, all represented in the garden of remembrance. I felt greatly honoured to be invited to humbly add the name of the Right Honourable Lord Provost of Glasgow, David Hodge, to this impressive roll of honour.

'It was quite unbelievable to see a tree bearing fruit, large and small, growing with oranges, limes, tangerines, lemons and grapefruit at one and the same time. The Russians had this idea of living things growing together in a spirit of peace and friendship.

'Unfortunately the world has not yet got the message, but we must live in hope that, one day, it will and people, not politicians, take over!

'May I add that, as our climate does not encourage the growing of citrus fruits, my graft was that of an orange which originated in California. It may take two years for a successful graft to produce any ripe fruit, so maybe the football team Dynamo Moscow will one day be sucking on one of my oranges at half-time during a game.'

David Hodge, former Lord Provost of Glasgow.

Reality Television

• • •

If, like me, you are fed up to the back teeth with reality TV shows, let me put forward a suggestion, as a former police officer, for a reality TV show that would be worth the licence fee.

Now, my personal pet hate is that shite they call *Big Brother* and the total diddies and unknown oddities they seem to audition for the show and who we, as the viewing public, are expected to watch, then phone up and vote for your favourite twat, who behaves like a toss-pot, in order for him or her to remain in the house.

The eventual last man standing, so to speak, gets a few boob – sorry – a few bob for surviving the tiaras and tantrums, the clothes on and clothes off, the exposed pierced nipples and tattooed torsos of pain-in-the-arse contestants loosely referred to as 'housemates'.

My idea to rival *Big Brother* would be to gather up a selected bunch of society's nutcases, bampots and disruptive unruly neds — we'll even introduce a few do-gooders — before conveying them all to Barlinnie prison, better known in Glasgow as the 'big house', and instead of 'housemates', we'll call them 'cellmates'.

Next thing would be to integrate them in the specific cell block reserved for convicted murderers, a few of whom are eager to make a name for themselves and hoping to write a bestseller afterwards, when crowned the *Big House Baddie*.

The 'Bar-L gang' will view the *BHB* TV tapes and decide the punishment for unpopular cellmates in the 'jail-house block'.

Heinous crimes – like squeezing the toothpaste at the

wrong end, not eating the vegetables on your plate, talking total bollocks in the exercise yard, boasting of sexual conquests and admitting live on air that you fancy Davina McCall – would immediately represent a nomination for the 'chop' by your new jury of cell-mate buddies!

Now, is that not worth watching?

The Spark-le is Still There

. . .

After twenty-five years of marriage, a police inspector surprised his wife by returning with her to the hotel where they had spent their first honeymoon night.

The following day, he drove her to an area near to a farmer's field where they had enjoyed their first romantic kiss!

They both got out of the car and, hand in hand, walked over to the special spot.

He took her in his arms and leaned her against the fence as he kissed her ever so passionately.

The wife suddenly responded in an erotic manner, digging her nails into his back, gripping him tightly and biting his face.

She then jumped up on him and wrapped her legs tightly around his waist, squeezing him as she yelled and squealed ecstatically.

The inspector's reaction was one of total sexual excitement: 'Darling, you weren't as amorous or vigorous as this twenty five years ago!'

The wife responded, 'No, and the farmer's fence wasn't electrified then either!!'

Surprise! Surprise!

· · ·

Dougie Mack was a cop with a mad passion for eating pie and beans. He adored them.

The only problem was they didn't particularly agree with him.

You see, after consuming a few pints of Guinness and a few greasy pies smothered in beans, he would suffer the most horrendous, obnoxious flatulence, in fact he was an out-and-out 'pongo'!

Suffice to say, wherever he go, the 'pongo'!

This did not unduly bother him, being a single bloke, until he met a policewoman and started dating her.

After dating for over a year, the inevitable happened and they got engaged and subsequently handcuffed – sorry, I mean married. (Same thing!)

Several months later, Dougie was involved in a big drugs-bust court case and, having obtained a conviction, he accompanied some of his fellow Drug Squad mates to a local hostelry for a bevvy session to celebrate.

After swallowing numerous pints of Guinness, Dougie the dutiful husband made his excuses and left to catch his bus home.

However, whilst standing at the bus stop awaiting its arrival, he could smell an aroma which had escaped his nostrils and taste buds for so long – yes, it was pie and beans!

The aroma to his nose was what Chanel No. 5 is to a woman – pure nectar from the gods.

As he stood there soaking up this bouquet of fragrance, he thought to himself, why not have just one?

One wouldn't hurt anybody and it would go a long way to satisfying his craving!

Finally convinced, he walked into the baker's shop and purchased one.

Oh, how he enjoyed it — three bites and it was gone. Suddenly it occurred to him that it was still quite early, so why not have another and he could walk part of the route home, ridding himself of any foul flatulence on the way. He could arrive home with his lovely wife none the wiser.

He talked himself into it and re-entered the shop.

The greedy pig didn't stop at one pie and before he left the shop he had scoffed three more. They hardly touched the sides of his throat on their way down.

Off he went along the road (wind-assisted), striding it out like a beat policeman, farting away like a four-bob rocket on Guy Fawkes Night, every few minutes – 'Bbbrrrpppp!'

It was like walking on Nike Air without wearing the trainers, as each step he took practically blew the backside out of his trousers. It was brilliant with no one to bother about. He was only a threat to local wildlife.

Finally, almost at his house, he'd passed enough wind to rewrite *The Wind in the Willows* and play the lead part in *The House at Pooh Corner*.

He had contaminated the entire countryside with his foul waste and with time left for one more blowout before he reached his front door.

He cocked his leg up to one side and – 'Bbbrrrpppp!'

He then paused for a moment, before minging – sorry, *ringing* – his doorbell!!!

After a few moments, his wife duly answered the door.

'Hello, darling!' she said as she leaned forward, placing a kiss on his cheek.

'Hello, love,' he responded. He stepped inside the hall and was about to remove his jacket when his wife said, 'Stop! Close your eyes, darling. I have a nice surprise for you!'

Being the obedient husband, he complied with her request.

She then led him along the hall with his eyes tightly closed and into the lounge area of the house.

'Right,' she said, 'on the count of three, I want you to open your eyes.' She began to count, 'One, two—' and before she could say 'three' the telephone rang.

'Stop! Don't open your eyes. Promise me you'll keep them closed until I return,' she pleaded with him.

'I promise, I promise!' he replied.

She went into the hallway to answer the telephone.

While awaiting her return, Dougie's stomach rumbled with a build-up of gas, which he had just got to get rid of – pronto!

He cocked his ear in the direction of his wife on the telephone and, hearing her engaged in conversation, he let rip – 'Bbbrrrpppp!'

What a rasper this was and he didn't even have a dog he could blame for it.

The smell was so strong you could practically taste it!

If it was canned it could be sold as insect repellent!

There were probably enough vitamins in it to cure a Mediterranean disease!

He began blowing frantically and waving his hands about in an effort to disperse the pong, still with his eyes closed tightly.

What a good husband (probably stinging anyway) – he was totally bowfin'!!

His wife called out to him from the hallway, 'I hope you still have your eyes closed tightly!'

Dougie shouted back, 'Yes, sweetie pie!'

There was nothing sweet about this pie and he knew it!

'I wouldn't want to spoil your surprise for me.'

He then quietly muttered to himself, 'I hope it's not pie and bloody beans.' He then giggled to himself nervously.

Suddenly, he felt another rumble in his stomach – surely not again!

He felt like he was about to lift off!

His bomb doors were about to open fully!

Was this a three-minute warning that the brownies were coming? Definitely!!

However, he couldn't go to the toilet because he would have to pass his wife in the hall.

Panic-stricken, he had a repeat of his last fart, only double and in stereo. 'Bbrrrpppp – brrrpppp!!' Uugghhh!!!

It felt as though he had just passed a bowling ball – whole! He was absolutely stinking!

He smelled as if he was in the advanced stages of decomposing.

Local farmers would pay him just to roll over and fertilise their fields.

The UN are searching Iraq for chemical weapons and here we have our very own located in a suburban estate in Glasgow!

This last one took the biscuit.

This time the bunnet was off his head and he was vigorously waving it about in front and behind him, in an effort to dilute the stench that he had produced.

Then panic as his wife finished off her telephone conversation.

He stopped his frantic waving and tried to act natural.

His wife entered the room and said, 'Right, did you open your eyes?'

'No, darling, I did not,' he replied. 'Honest!'

'Good,' said the wife. 'Well, you can open them now!'

Very slowly, he opened his eyes and gasped in horror, as seated around the room were police colleagues, friends and relatives, who in unison, burst into song: 'Happy Birthday to you!!! Happy Birthday to you!!!'

'Aaaarrrrgggghhhhh!!!'

My Appreciation

. . .

The author would like to thank you for buying this book and hopes that you had as much fun reading it, as he had writing and compiling it.

The author would also like to thank the many police colleagues/characters who made it possible to write about all this but impossible to tell the real truth.

The author would also like to add that most of the names have been changed to protect the guilty and most of the stories have been exaggerated!

The Harry the Polis cartoons were created and written by Harry Morris and illustrated by Derek Seal.

Harry Morris, who appears courtesy of his parents, is available as an after dinner speaker for functions and can be contacted by email at:

harry.morris51@virgin.net.

Or by post:

PO BOX 7031, GLASGOW, G44 3YN. SCOTLAND.